The Bad Dad's Survival Guide

The Bad Dad's Survival Guide

Adam Brophy

Gill & Macmillan

Gill & Macmillan Ltd
Hume Avenue, Park West, Dublin 12
with associated companies throughout the world
www.gillmacmillan.ie

978 07171 4556 0

Illustrations by Neil Ardiff
Typography design by Make Communication
Print origination by O'K Graphic Design, Dublin
Printed by ColourBooks Ltd, Dublin

This book is typeset in 11/14 pt Minion.

The paper used in this book comes from the wood pulp of
managed forests. For every tree felled, at least one tree is planted,
thereby renewing natural resources.

A CIP catalogue record for this book is available from the
British Library.

5 4 3 2 1

For Nell and Mia

Contents

Acknowledgements

Every first-time author thanks the world, his mammy and his childhood sweetheart; we're a skittish bunch. I'll try to be brief.

First off, in *The Irish Times* Fionnuala Mulcahy published an unsolicited article of mine on the perils of fatherhood back in 2006. That got my gums flapping. Sheila Wayman gave me a column on the back of it and Hugh Linehan and Barry O'Keefe kept that column going. Thank you all.

The good people in Gill & Macmillan have been a pleasure to work with, which might not surprise you, the reader, but I used to work there soo … aaahm … well … I'll shut up now. Fergal, D, Teresa, Emily and Nicki, cheers.

Diarmaid Ferriter, Paul McCormack and Cian Hogan read an early draft and told me not to be ridiculous about any number of things. And they were right. In some instances I ignored them, instances identifiable by their ridiculousness. Neil Ardiff came on board at short notice and drew me up some damn fine cartoons. Good man, Neil!

All my original learnings about fatherhood came, of course, from my old man. Kevin Brophy was my first exposure to a 'Bad Dad' and Mary Brophy showed me how a woman has to deal with one. Thanks Mum. Thanks Dad.

But most of all, I need to thank my three girls: Cathy, Nell and Mia. You are a constant source of inspiration and perspiration. Living with you guys reminds me how little I really know despite thinking I know it all. More importantly, it reminds me that how little I know is of little importance as long as we keep rattling along together.

Adam Brophy
January 2009

Chapter 1

Conception

SCENARIO 1—JIM

It's about 8.30 on Saturday night. You're on the couch trawling through the satellite channels, settling in for a half hour of *Only Fools and Horses* on Dave when the mobile goes. Rumours of a party in Portobello later, drinks first in town. You mumble ambiguously, you're tired after the skinful last night, but eventually a commitment is wheedled out of you. You'll be in town by ten.

As you rise from the couch, like an elephant seal lurching towards the water, the Domino's box falls to the floor, spilling crusts, undesired onions and sweet chilli sauce containers on to the carpet. You look vaguely at the mess, knowing it's going to stain, wondering will it affect your deposit.

Leave it there, she might tidy it tomorrow. If she's talking to you.

You grab a towel, throw off the nine-year-old robe that's warmed you all day and advance towards the *en suite*. *En suite* me swiss, when they tagged this on to the bedroom it was probably to cover the exposed sewage pipe that was close enough to cuddle from your scratcher. When the two of you looked at the place originally you both marvelled at how cute it was. It's not so cute now that she's fully commandeered the main bathroom and you're under fixed and stern instruction not to deviate from your waterpress. It's not so cute performing contortions at 4 a.m. as the previous night's curry and lager makes a swift and shock exit.

The shower works in that it expels water. Sometimes hot, usually cold. And hopefully the damp patch forming on the bedroom wall adjacent to the cubicle won't result in structural collapse before your lease runs its course. Christ, the place is four years old and feels Dickensian.

The water rouses you. Afterwards, you shave using Geo F Trumper shaving cream which allows your Mach IV to glide as smoothly as possible with no chance of a nick. It's Stg£14 a tub online but so worth it, the supermarket brands you can pick up in the shop leave your face looking like a brazzer's slapped arse.

Once your face has been picked clean, you immediately spray it with a fine mist of Dr Hauschka facial toner. This is usually marketed as a woman's product, but more and more of the lads are recognising it for its invigorating properties. Its witch-hazel and kidney vetch ingredients combine to stimulate the natural moisturising process, making it the ideal shave/moisturise crossover product. Again not cheap, you pick it up in BT for €26 for 100 mls but the girls on the counter know you and throw in the odd sampler to minimise wallet dentage.

Moisturising is essential. A fact you noted immediately when, on the night of your twentieth-eighth birthday, some UCD Arts honey commented on your lines being full of character. You did your homework and after some trial and error settled on Botanical Kinetics Hydrating Lotion by Aveda. It leaves your skin feeling moisture-refreshed and offers powerful protection from the type of dehydration best inflicted by overcrowded bars and clubs. It's an expense, but the most important one of all; this is the baby to have you looking thirty at forty and cruising into the night. And you've discovered a guy on eBay who must have a warehouse full of the stuff. He's been supplying you for a year now at about half the RRP. Where he got it—who really cares? Goat's milk to the skin.

The phone's beeping, three texts. All of them from Stan—'Don't be late', 'You're a prick' and, just for good measure, 'Bent'.

Tonight's going to be joe average. Nothing formal, nothing glitzy. Camper leather trainers (brown), Hilfiger jeans (boot fit), Armani T-shirt, Tag Heuer classic on the wrist and you'll dust down the Stone Island jacket for the first night of winter. It's been getting chilly lately. You kick through last week's clobber on the floor to admire yourself in the full-length dressmaker's mirror you picked up for a song at auction in Buckley's in Glasthule. Looking nice, but you're not happy with the staying power of your Fudge Hair Putty and resolve to go back to Lock Stock and Barrel—The Daddy Classic Wax. It just takes you through the night.

Gear on, face on, quick bell to the missus. 'All right? Where are you?'

'Nearys. Karen's last night before heading for Oz. Remember, I told you about it this afternoon?'

No, you didn't. 'Right, yeah. I'm off into the Stag's. Probably straight up to Jimmy's after, some sort of party on.'

'Yeah, I know. I told you about it this afternoon. We'll be up after Hogan's chucks out. Do you remember anything I said to you today?'

'Course I do darling. You said you couldn't believe your luck every time you stared at my Adonis like figure and realised you got to bring me home for keeps.'

'Yeah, I did. Are you going to keep it tidy tonight?'

'Within reason. You?'

'Might make an effort. Just promise me one thing. You won't invite every stray back to ours when Jimmy's making kicking out noises, okay? I don't want a repeat of last time. Phil is not welcome in our place, he isn't housetrained.'

'No worries, we'll be grand. I'll see you up there, right. Don't be too late. Love ya.'

The phone beeps again. Stan's latest text: 'You haven't left the house yet. Prick.'

———

The Stag's Head. It's had the same faces mingling between random tourists for as long as you can remember. You've been coming here since you could get served. It's home. Even a change of ownership, while admittedly upsetting, hasn't resulted in it being dethroned. The downstairs is now officially too vulgar for consideration but you had long since given up going down there anyway. Dublin

Literary Crawl American tourists squeezed in listening to trad pap. Good luck. But upstairs you still have a dependable pint. The new owner read the lay of the land and chucked in some quality east European totty too. You don't order a pint from them at the bar, but you'll happily have one dropped down.

The lads are seated deep in the corner ensuring no interlopers sneak in. You look at them and know if you met most of them now you'd keep on walking. But loyalty is important, tradition is important, they are where you're from, they are what you are, there is safety in the familiar. And the familiar is always good to come home to.

A couple of hours there covers that day's results cross-channel, the appalling state of the national rugby team, who's lashing who out of it, or more pertinently, who's not, and the latest brushes with controversy and/or the law. Work is not mentioned, neither are official partners. Sex is acceptable when it involves parties none of you have been overly familiar with and so explicit details are not only allowed but actively encouraged. Those of you in long-term relationships savour the revelations, the successful conquerors gloat, the involuntary chaste wallow. This plays out in every boozer across the known universe every Saturday night.

The pace accelerates. The next boozer, it may be Kehoe's, it may not, passes by in a parade of grinning, leering faces, uproarious laughter, back slapping and increased demands to 'get the round in'. You're up and down to the bar, in and out of the stall. You're banging along, you're the funniest fucker around. On to the party.

There's a cab ride, there's Jimmy's house, music, familiar faces. It's all good, bro. The missus collars you and admonishes you for your mental weakness. But she's not looking too hot herself, even if that's just down to a long line of voddie and red bull. She grins and accepts the pill you place on her tongue.

The music rises. The tribe swamps the kitchen, forms lines, swaying, smiling, stomping. Hands in the air, we're all here, we're all great. This is it, this is all that matters, us together, together, together, friends together. Cheers go up as a big one segues in, mix it back, bring it up, up to where we are, all high, all together. We're all here.

'Right, get out the lot of yiz. That's your lot.'

The crowd moans.

'Don't mind him. It's all back to mine. Who's got skins?'

———

'Ah, move over love will ya.' She always does this, takes the whole bed up when you need space more than ever. You crack an eye and realise it's Stan that's suffocating you. His face is two inches from yours. You slap him, he wakes. You tell him to shift his lardy arse and he looks like he's got the hump. But he moves.

You sit up and drain the pint of water at your bedside. Stan's left the door to the living room open and you can see at least three bodies in there. You see him pick up an old can, drain it, settle on a chair and start to build a spliff. He catches your eye and nods questioningly. You shake your head, heave out of bed and shut the door. Hell to pay later.

One long siphon in the press and you're back in bed. It's warm, you're delicate. The Solpadeine's in the kitchen, much too far away. You nudge her and she mumbles. You nudge her again, this time with no hands. She presses back into you but doesn't open an eye. You reach under her top and give her a squeeze. The romance. Within ten minutes you're dozing again.

———

Six weeks later.

'What the fuck! What the fuck! What the fuck?'

She's standing in the doorway of the waterpress. Typical, when she has to pee on a stick she uses your bathroom. You can see the little blue line from where you're lying.

'How did this happen? You prick. What the fuck did you do?'

Not the most auspicious of starts for the poor little blighter.

SCENARIO 2—FRANK

It's about 8.30 on a Saturday morning. You're lying, still snug, in your emperor size, hand-made sleigh bed visualising that morning's run. Six miles at seven-minute pace, a significant increase but you need to lower your base speed if you're to have a chance of beating your PB in this year's London marathon. If you clear the points of difficulty in your morning route, in advance, in your mind, you can attack them without fear later, in reality.

She turns beside you and moves her head onto your shoulder. Her hand slips onto your chest and pulls at the hair there.

'I'm ready, this is the morning. My chart says we should do it before we get up. Apparently my egg is gasping for you right now.'

'Oh man, are you serious? You know I'm supposed to run.'

She's up on one elbow; the stern look is on. The one that whipped you into a frenzy when it was employed with stilettos, PVC, handcuffs and a whip some years back. Now, it's only ever for keeps. She wants it, she gets it.

The look says, 'Don't fuck with me. We've been through this. Everything is right, right now. If we don't have a child within the next eighteen months we could miss our window of opportunity for optimum financial stability coupled with maximum adult/ child face time.'

She repeats threateningly, 'We've been through this.'

She's right—you have.

The sex is robust but mechanical, two people used to being in charge working towards a common goal. It's just unfortunate that that common goal is no longer mutual pleasure, now it is an addition to your unit, something to make you seem worthwhile. So then, maybe it is mutual pleasure, except deferred to the long term. Like a pension plan, or an architect-designed extension, or an aggressively-managed hedge fund.

Your seed is sent on its way, the soldiers fighting for supremacy to forge to the front and lay waste that egg's defences. The egg sits there, prim and faultless, assured in its perfection, yet to be tarnished. Urging those soldiers on.

You've been trying for months. No joy. You barely speak any more except to ensure your paths cross in times of fertility. If relations are strained at home, they are crackling at work. Your team of Executive Finance Advisors have fallen short of target three quarters in a row. Where once everything you touched turned, if not to gold, then at least to deposits on a couple of investment properties and a minimum of two skiing holidays a year, now suddenly there is a waft of shit about your decisions. There is an air of concern within the office, but it is on a national level, nothing personal. The economy has turned, people are waiting for opportunity, there is a lull.

But you have taken it personally. You can't make money, for yourself or other people. You curse your team and placate your boss, when there is no reason for either. Situations are spiralling beyond your control and you can't sit and allow nature take its course; you should be able to fix it because up to now you always have.

Your hair is thinning, you've gotten a little loose around the middle, that long jaw-line is displaying a sag at its midpoint. You've stopped playing rugby and taken up distance running because it hurts less.

You can't get your wife pregnant.

More A's than B's in your Leaving Cert which you sat in one of south Dublin's most prestigious rugby nurseries got you into university. A Commerce degree from UCD and an MBA from the Smurfit School of Business, a first and a distinction respectively. Recruited by KPMG on graduation you cut your teeth in London and Tokyo. But five years later you got hauled home by Bank of Ireland with a lucrative offer which had your father's fingerprints all over it.

Within six months of settling back in you met Rachel, the younger sister of an old buddy from the SCT and it was a real case of horses for courses from there on in. She was forging through McCann Fitzgerald, making corporate law look sexy, very sexy.

Once the initial discomfort of scoring your buddy's sibling was appeased it was a free for all in the trouser department, both of you fighting for who got to wear them. And occasionally you were willing enough to swap apparel, comfortable as you both were in your own sexuality. The first year was such a trail of wanton carnage that you came close to losing friends. Who would want to sit through rambling dull dinners with half-interesting acquaintances when you could be at home knocking the slapped arses off each other? She liked a little slap back then, a lusty cuff to the left buttock. As you did yourself.

But soon reality edges in. Friday night rendezvous become unnecessary when she has her own key, then her own drawer, then she's in. She lets out her two-bed in the Winter Gardens and you set up shop in your three-bed in Ranelagh as it's that bit more spacious. Living together is tolerated by both families, a common enough jape these days, but the ring goes on her finger sharpish. Her dad's needling had an edge to it that was not to be taken lightly. He is a man not to be taken lightly. She has not fallen far from the tree.

The wedding is a lush affair. A guest list of 250, ice swans, Moët on tap and one VIP arrival by helicopter. She gushes it is the best day of her life. It passes in a blur for you. Honeymoon in Mauritius and back home with a dictat from both your and her father for you to make serious cash and for her to produce some blue-eyed offspring.

That was two years ago. The cash hadn't been a problem until recently and neither had the kids. But the cracks are beginning to show. You've suffered bouts of tendonitis in both knees which the physio puts down to over-training but which you are smart enough to realise is stress-related. And still no sign. No yearned-for morning sickness, no joyous, hand-held presentation of the good news to the families. No little bastard to get everybody off your goddamn back.

She has tried relaxation, meditation and yoga (both Ashtanga and Vinyasa Flow). You have come home to moon charts and sea tables plotting the pull of the earth. Your diet is so fresh you would have to nuzzle your own muzzle into the earth for it to improve. You have ingested a parade of homeopathic remedies, herbal essences and foul-smelling Chinese concoctions. And still no baby.

She has three sisters and a brother. You are an only child. It's obviously your fault. You don't need some Mater Private stalwart to tell you that. What's wrong with your seed?

Then one morning, one Monday morning, you're putting your bag together for the ten o'clock briefing before making the twenty-minute stroll into the office when she comes screaming down the stairs. She launches at you, sobbing, and you only just manage to catch her, and it's then, when she's telling you that she had had a feeling that this would be the month, that you realise she had been even more concerned about this whole thing than you. From the kitchen you can hear Hard-Fi singing 'Cash Machine' on the radio: 'My girlfriend's just turned blue, What am I gonna do?'

Not a problem for you mate, all your troubles are over. Here comes baby and everything is going to be all right.

———

There seems to be a generalised response to being told you are about to become a father, among Irish men anyway. I'd go so far as to spread that to the UK, mainland Europe and North America. The rest of the world I can't vouch for, they're all rather strange anyway.

Having survived the first forays into the wonderland that is sexual exploration in your teens without suffering the disaster of 'unwanted teen pregnancy', most of us seem to internalise the terror of actually procreating through the act of procreation. So, no matter how much we desire to have a child, no matter how secure we are, financially, emotionally, physically even (it always helps to have a strong back), when the words 'I'm pregnant' are uttered to us for the first time, we have some measure of a tremor.

For some that fear takes hold and is overwhelming, for others it is quickly blown aside by joy. Whatever the situation, the fear comes first and has a nibble. Whether joy is immediately subsequent is variable but, sure as your days of easy lays are numbered, the sense of relief kicks in immediately afterwards.

You're not shooting blanks, you're all man, there's ammo in your cannon, you're a big blue-balled stallion. Go shout it from the mountain tops: 'Know what, world? I can make babies! With me mickey! How about that?'

Note the swagger in a prospective new father's walk. That's the walk of a man who has had to adjust to making room in his pants for something with a bit of extra presence. He never knew it before but he's a magician, he can create human beings with that wand down there, which up until now had only caused him ongoing frustration interspersed with moments, blessed moments, of relief. That wand marks him out as a testosterone-oozing bang merchant. Don't walk too close, honey, do you know what I can do to you with this thing here? Don't you know I'm all man?

That's the sad fact of it all. We do what creatures have been doing since the first Big Bang and we think we're special. We're good at this; if we have a cold it's probably the Ebola virus. We like to think we're restrained alpha males and, but for the lack of opportunity, we should be sitting in the Oval Office running the free world. We succeed at one of our basest instincts, surpassed only by the need to feed our fat faces, and think we've proved something. We've provided a lucky world with a reproduction of ourselves.

Fear followed by relief followed by pride. We are told we are to become parents and that's our response. The thing is, each of those emotions is for our *own* state of being. We are fearful immediately that something is coming to mess with our lives, to deny us our free will. We are relieved that we can bray at strangers that we have the power to turn paste into people. We are proud that another version of our own hardly fantastic selves will be around into the distant future to have another chance at getting right all the things we so magnificently fucked up.

We are so dumb that any governing body with a gram of common sense coupled with public decency would sterilise us for the good of the planet and the small friendly animals that live on it. Because we shouldn't be allowed to have babies. Because we are blokes and we have our heads in our asses and we like the view

there. We experience all these emotions for ourselves at the imminent arrival of the next generation, when all that next generation demands is every bit of our time, love, attention, care and, most of all, wallet. Our blue line response and subsequent bath in single malt scotch is about the last time we get to respond in an emotional way that is purely our own. The emotional response we have developed since birth, which is to think with pure concern for ourselves alone and occasionally the piece of tackle that hangs between our legs with an agenda all of its own, is to be whacked aside first by the mother and then by that ever-hungry child.

We think we have stamped our mark on the world. We think we have secured our dynasty, ensured our lineage and ongoing legacy. What we have done is nailed down the lids of our coffins, we have only to spend the rest of our days scratching at them from the inside, desperately trying to get out. We have voluntarily given it all up in the vain and deluded belief that this is the right path. We wave our little certificate of pregnancy like Neville Chamberlain on his return from Germany in 1939. 'Peace In Our Time?' I think not.

It doesn't matter how you got to this point, whether it was through a military operation of astutely-timed precision or from a head-aching drink and drug-fuelled recovery fumble, the fact is that you are here now. At the starter's blocks, about to set out on a long trudge of a race without a map or a manual to your name. Left holding nothing but your dick in your hand, and you might want to yank that off for a start to avoid any further trouble. But let's call that the nuclear option and crack on with what might work out in the long term. Here and now, you're in big trouble. If you don't plan a far-sighted and progressive strategy, the parts of life that you enjoyed until now are joining the *Titanic* at the bottom of a cold and dark man ocean. A place populated by discarded weekends to Ibiza, afternoons in front of the premiership and short-lived hobbies of the saxophone variety. Your choices, your options are gone.

Unless you make provision.

Unless you plan your survival.

Chapter 2
Pregnancy

THE FIRST TRIMESTER: THE FAÇADE OF NORMALITY

Take a look at your pregnant wife or girlfriend. It doesn't much matter how you address her, she appears much the same as she ever has. To the uneducated eye she is human; she's the funny-faced, googly-eyed girl you fell for, the one who could pull you out of your Sunday evening work-fear slump. The one who made you laugh so hard while out drinking together that you'd half puke, half backwash your lager into your glass. Then she'd dare you to drink it.

This is the girl you lied to your friends for, just so you could chill with her and her mates instead of spending the afternoon watching premiership football in the dark confines of the Leeson Lounge on a Saturday afternoon. You've gone shopping with her. Voluntarily. You've gone bra shopping with her. You've had many weekend breaks, you've chilled by the pool together on fortnight packages to Fuengirola, you've travelled together, maybe seen Vietnam or trekked the Inca Trail.

Now look at her again. If she smiles, take a quick gander at her teeth. Is there any noticeable sharpening of the incisors? Anything to suggest that the saliva coating her tongue has changed to acid? If you study her carefully can you make out the deepened lines that may suggest the furrowed brows demonstrated so carefully by the monsters in the *Buffy The Vampire Slayer* series?

Of course you can't, you muppet. And you know why? Because this is no simple case of demonic possession. To deal with this you can't ring up William Peter Blatty and shout down the blower at him, 'Oi, Billy, where do you get your exorcists then?' I don't know if Mr Blatty has kids of his own, but if he does he will be among the band of brothers that knows an exorcist will do you no good here. For now, like all generations before you, you are in the presence of the most insidious type of possession. This is a demon that creeps and grows in the light, one that you invited in, one that bears your own genetic code. This monster in your child's mother's smooth-skinned frame is the one that operates under the moniker of reproduction.

As your 'good news' filters through friends and family there will be many comments, witty asides and ascerbic warnings. Chief among these is the grizzly insight that 'There's three of you now, young man. Time to clip your wings and think about the future. You're a family man from here on in.'

Leaving aside the innate depression that people love to spread which involves wishing a lifetime of misery on you simply because you've knocked your bird up, this little gem of wisdom is pure bullshit. If the only people involved in your latest life step were you, her and the forthcoming progeny the future would be so much more manageable. The trouble comes because of the hooded invader, the one that steals into your nuclear family unannounced and possesses the woman that until now you have cherished. There aren't three of you involved here, your brood has grown to a minimum of four. You, her, it or them (please God not twins—go on, chant it for safety) and the pregnancy demon. Many people know of this creature but none will acknowledge it.

You must spend your time with the beast. Your woman remains, in fact because of the baby growing in her she will appear, despite some physical maladies, even more buoyant and physical than ever. Her possession is subtle and intangible and her possessor's sole purpose is to use her as a vessel to attack you. Preparation and an understanding of the biological process taking place are vital. I'm no doctor, but reading about the physical symptoms of the first trimester helped me come to terms with the extremity of changes in the apparently unaltered creature beside me.

The first four weeks after you satisfied your urges and sowed your valued man-seed involve the fusion of sperm and egg into a one-celled entity, a zygote. If more than one egg frees up you could have a couple of zygotes involved. God bless you. The zygote contains forty-six chromosomes, retained equally from you and the missus. As these determine sex, physical and personality traits, as well as intelligence, you should probably hope this is one time her presence overpowers yours.

By week four you have an embryo in there. It may only be 1/25th of an inch long but it's making its presence felt. The spine is starting to shape up, a primitive circulatory system is pulling itself together and the cell formation of the major organs is buzzing along. The following week the heart starts to beat, and when the heart's involved you know there's trouble close behind.

The growth in her womb speeds up in week six. It has tripled in size in a fortnight, the heart is banging with regularity and facial features start to appear with a mouth opening and passageways that will make up the inner ear. The digestive and respiratory systems are beginning to form, along with blocks of tissue that will develop into ribs and muscles and small buds destined to become arms and legs.

You see her mooching around the place, licking pieces of coal and demanding grass-flavoured ice-cream and all you can think is, 'Woohoo! A free breast lift, fantastic! All I did was give her the good love. Yes sir, solo high five!' You daft prick, there's a body in there, already taking shape, he just hasn't pushed out the sides of his parcel yet. You haven't been overwhelmed by her morning sickness because you've been fixated by her new, natural implants. But it's time to wake up, to get with what's going on. If you come to some morning and she's about to stab you in the eye with an ice-pick it's because you haven't been paying attention.

By week seven the umbilical cord is clearly visible, the arms are looking like little paddles and the nose, mouth and ears are getting clearer. A few days later and you have ankles and webbed fingers and toes. The heart is cracking along at around 150 beats a minute; that's going to need some serious fuel.

In week nine you can make out a tadpole. The head is about half the size of the whole, which, while you want the lad or lassie to grow up reasonably bright, isn't a good look. The rest of the organs begin to form and the baby may begin to start shifting around, though there won't be any discomfort (from his efforts) to Mum just yet. He's still too small to cause physical pain, give him time.

By now fingers and toes have fully separated so your baby, thankfully, is more human than fish. To add to this manifestation of humanity, the bones of his skeleton have begun to form. More importantly, if your baby is a boy his testes will start producing testosterone. It is not known if he is yet a slave to this development, but as the majority of his life will be based on making rash decisions due to this natural phenomenon, we would hope he would have a brief respite from the pain those urges will cause him. Freud never paid much attention to pre-natal psychology but if he did he would probably suggest that it is about now that baby develops x-ray vision and starts to instruct Mum to kick Dad out of bed while cosying up a little obscenely to her internal organs.

A week later and baby's place in the world is set in stone as external genitalia develop into a recognisable penis or clitoris and labia majora. Then, twelve weeks into pregnancy, the end of the first trimester, baby reaches about three inches and weighs somewhere close to 4/5 of an ounce. This week is also marked by the arrival of fingernails and toenails.

All the better for scratching you with, my dear.

This time is hard for guys. Without any real, outward, physical signs that much change is afoot we struggle to come to terms with a very definitely, suddenly skewed playing field.

First, the ecstasy. The 'Oh my God, I'm gonna be a mother.' After blue-line day there are the promises that nobody should be told until twelve weeks have passed. You will be warned that it is bad luck for anyone to know before this time has passed as a large percentage of pregnancies 'self-terminate' during that time. That phrase 'self-terminate' is rotten, but as we accompany the mother down this road there are many word groupings to be learned that we probably never expected to utter. Self-terminate implies the little blighter decided the time wasn't right and he was going to avoid the whole pregnancy, birth and living drama. Some strands of psychology will agree with this perspective but it implies an innate consciousness of the soulful/less, spiritual variety.

A baby dies during the early stages of pregnancy. That's what happens. The baby dies and both parents feel its loss. They may never have known the child but they lose one and feel it strongly, sometimes wondering why they are affected by the event so much. The medical phrase 'self-termination', like many of its ilk, dehumanises what has happened in an insensitive attempt to normalise a common occurrence. It may be common but it is no less traumatic. When a child dies at this premature stage everybody still grieves. Unfortunately there are few support systems in place to comfort parents who have to deal with this scenario; instead they are shoved back out into the world and encouraged to have another shot at it. If that were done when a child died shortly after birth it would be deemed inhumane, yet in this situation it is regarded as pointless to grieve the passing of one who had so briefly been part of the family. The issue of when a fetus becomes an embryo and becomes a person is much debated in philosophical circles and vitriolic pro- and anti-abortion head to heads, but the point is that when a parent suffers the death of a child at any stage, it hurts. The father, although not physically involved, suffers too.

And this all started in such a light-hearted manner. But it may be the source of the twelve-week Omerta that is generally inflicted on the father. Off he goes, carrying his terror at the world being whipped from under him, with this irrational fear that if he does in fact whisper a word to a soul he may endanger in some voodoo way the life of his unborn child. He goes to work and immediately has a panic attack when he realises that they can't survive on a pair of salaries when there's only two in the house—what's he going to do when there's another screaming maw to feed? Even Frank in scenario two of Chapter 1 experiences the initial baby terror, but he more than anyone else can't break the twelve-week rule. Everybody and their maiden aunt knows how long they've been trying for this news; if he were to jinx it now the vice would tighten around his nuts in Inquisition-style perpetuity.

Of course, immediately after extracting this promise from the fearful male, Mum has rung in sick to work and screamed across town to let her mother be the first to know she is to be a granny. Apart, that is, from the girl who handed her a free paper at the city centre traffic lights and the newsagent who sold her the last packet of cigarettes she would ever smoke. She couldn't help but tell them, the excitement was just welling up in her, don't you know!

Dad makes his way home numb with fear that night. It vaguely registers that everyone he passes en route smiles benignly and winks but it is only when he picks up a copy of the *Evening Herald* and sees the full-page announcement on the back page to his powers of procreativity that he realises he has been duped. It is the first of many harsh lessons.

Then begins the merry roundabout of telling friends and relatives. Work really does wait because you have to be sure of predicted birth dates, just so Mum can alter them slightly in order that maternity leave be scheduled to begin on the very morning the child appears. No point in wasting valuable paid time-off at home with a belly like a beer keg, piles the size of apricots and no company but Jerry Springer. That time should be spent in front of your office PC, sweating and explaining how it's highly unrealistic for anyone to expect you to do any work. Unless they're willing to rub your bunions and fan you simultaneously. Otherwise, 'Step off, bitch!'

But more about the third trimester later.

It's as the social whirl escalates that the sickness begins to take hold. They call it morning sickness, but morning now apparently extends to afternoons, evenings and especially when you're in a deep sleep around midnight. In some contemporary Western cultures it is called 'Get Me My Pepperoni Ice-cream and Athlete's Foot Flavoured Tea While You Rub My Back and Hold My Hair Out Of My Face As I Puke' sickness. But I hear they're socially advanced with wonderful health benefits in those countries. Here, it's a low growl, a contemptuous stare and a 'why can't you read my mind?' demand that has you on your toes for these joyous first few months.

The sickness is reserved for you. When the girls come round it is referred to with a witty delight, as if it is a minor infringement on your shared life together. Your ineptitude at helping her through her discomfort will become common currency in the humiliation she wishes to bestow upon you in return for inflicting such gastric horror on her. Take the abuse—you cannot fight this rage. Excuse yourself, phone friends, go to the pub and cry in public for the first time since primary school. Your mates' attempted lacerations will be no more cutting than a relaxing oiled back massage in comparison to the whipping you'll have been taking at home.

There are positives here. You are getting murdered behind closed doors. Outwardly, she is a delight, regaling visitors with her plans for the nursery, her thoughts on a natural childbirth (again, too much to cope with this here, see the next chapter), childcare implications, primary and secondary schools, the whole nature versus nurture philosophical argument. As with all first-time mothers, she is suddenly the world's foremost authority on all things childbirth and all societal implications therein. Dare you disagree? You are the whipping boy for her unspoken fears, which seem to boil down to the physical realisation that a bowling ball is set to pass through a cricket ball sized orifice that until now has only been used for pleasure seeking. And this is to happen in the not too distant future.

There is opportunity in adversity. Things can hardly be made worse for you. Take to drinking at unsociable hours. So what if you don't quite manage to make it home a couple of nights. This to the outside world would be seen as heartless, cruel even, but she won't allow the father of her child to be seen in that light and so is unlikely to make public your misdemeanours. You have a clear and inviting playing surface, one that will not be available for long. Eat spicy foods and leave the cartons strewn throughout the house, watch pornography in the knowledge that what you are preparing to witness will be far more vivid and imaginative, smoke bongs and tell your boss to back off when he comments on the Piccalilli stain on the white shirt you've worn for three consecutive days. He'll either understand or she'll ring your wife for the inside track.

If this is not quite your death knell as fancy free, it is close to a last hurrah. The difficulty is in enjoying your indulgence as it flies in the face of everything you are being told to do, i.e. be supportive, caring, loving, healthy, forward looking and productive. But come on, you have a kid on the way and no instructions, it's up to you whose rules you choose to follow.

By the end of the first trimester her sickness, with any luck, will have passed and you may be a shell of a man. In any three-month cycle, prolonged abuse, both of the self and from another, will have consequences. There will be a sense of fear, inevitable at the impending arrival, but also that you may have acquired some difficult habits to give up. There may be a feeling of hopelessness; your railing at the demands required of you might have provided you with an unseemly insight into the depths of selfishness you can sink to. There could be deep fatigue and a settled depression. Never mind, a part of the hard part has ended. The newness of the situation has vanished. What is happening is now common currency, your elevation from 'useless tart' among your closest friends to 'drivelling father-in-waiting' is complete.

She too is over the exhilaration and fear and entering a period of acceptance. This is fortunate, because at any other period of your lives together you would probably have been thrown out on your ear, if not thrown in the river by her father and brothers, for your behaviour over the preceding couple of months. But now you are entering what is known in pregnancy circles as 'The Enlightenment'. You must make hay while the sun shines, because it may be dark for many moons after this three months.

THE SECOND TRIMESTER: BLOOMING AND BUSTY

If you're lucky, and we're going to concentrate on the positive here as always, this is your window of opportunity. But having said that, we should, just for a second, spare a thought for the less fortunate.

Enjoyment of the second trimester, for both parents, depends on the sickness passing. In some cases this doesn't happen. It is not unheard of for the sickness to intensify and the mother to take to her bed for the remainder of her pregnancy. If that is the case,

there isn't much hope. You are set to spend six months waiting hand and foot on an entity that is eternally growing yet simultaneously being eaten from the inside. This entity will be driven by a combination of nausea and despair, disillusioned that this is the way her pregnancy is destined to turn out. You will bear the brunt of this.

There are two things to consider here. The first is that this will at least prepare you for dealing with an infant, which is a huge shock to all first-time fathers. The anger of a bedridden mother-to-be may not quite match the primal scream of a newborn. But it's as close as you'll get in everyday adult life. So, see your domestic jail time as valuable preparation.

The second is more tenuous. All pregnancies place great strains on relationships. This interim period where, for a short while, you actually like each other again was probably designed in evolutionary terms so that mother and father would have some idea as to why they got together in the first place, and therefore might have some designs on staying together after the child is born. If this brief time of reconciliation is denied, it will be a struggle to see anything positive in the other. One member of the pair is possessed while the other is beholden to the deranged creature. How you come back from that, I don't know. Some do, others spend the rest of their lives together frozen in these unnatural positions, one of supplicant, the other the aggressor. Throw a couple of kids into that mix and you have one angry, resentful family. The type you see simmering in its own juices as they 'enjoy' a Sunday lunch together in a mid-range, buffet carvery. In short, you want the sickness to at least ease when you hit the second trimester.

To demonstrate how this can be a time for unbridled joy for many the father, this may be an opportune moment to re-examine the situations our heroes from Chapter 1 find themselves in.

SCENARIO 1—JIM
You sit staring at the TV, a mug of tea gone cold in your hand. A re-run of *The Sopranos* flickers at you from the set. You're

considering one of the cans in the fridge but don't know if you can muster the energy to follow through. You've been drinking hard for six weeks now, since it became apparent there wasn't a whole lot else worth doing, and you're tired of it. It may be Friday, but what you'd really like is to order a pizza, rent a DVD, turn the phone off and snuggle for the night. The chance would be a fine thing.

You hear a key turn in the door and your body tenses in apprehension. Without any encouragement it adopts a war footing as soon as she approaches these days—you never know where the attack will come from and you've learned to be prepared. You wish now you had the beer in your hand, just to appear gamey, instead of the crumpled rag you feel like.

In she comes, saddled with paper bags of shopping. She gives you a glance and you wait for the barrage of abuse for not having vacuumed the place. It doesn't happen. She moves through to the kitchen and dumps the bags on the table. It's a small place, you know you're on display so you never lets your air of nonchalance down.

She slots everything away, filling fridge, freezer (well, ice-box really) and cupboards. You are a statue on the couch. Eventually she rests her hands on the table and looks over. 'You all right babe?' she asks. 'Would you like a beer?'

What new angle is this? What demented torture has she in mind with this sympathetic posturing? You want to grunt that you'll get it yourself, stroll by and fall back in situ without a care. But you wonder is it possible ... could she be genuine? You half-eyeball her and nod, non-committal. You wait.

'D'you wanna glass?'

'Nah, can is fine.'

She settles beside you and hands you the drink. For a minute you don't know what to do with your mug of cold tea and consider just tossing it over the back of the seat, so startled are you at this display of hospitality. But normality resumes, you place it on the coffee table and crack the brew.

'What are you watching?'

'*The Sopranos*, series two I think. The one where the boys clip

"Big Pussy" Bonpensiero,' you reply.

'Ah, I love that one. Tony at his sociopathic best.'

'You better believe it, babes. If only they did work placement schemes in the Mob when we were in Transition Year.'

This is normal. This is nice. You are bantering. Your body starts to relax but is still on low-grade alert for the disguised ambush.

'I miss you,' she says. 'I miss this.' Then she starts crying, slow, breathy sobs and she climbs onto your lap and hugs you. You manage to get your beer onto the arm of the couch and hug her back. 'I was in work today and for the first time in nearly three months I didn't have to make a dash for the toilets and spew my guts. Then I realised I was going to be able to eat lunch. And after that I nearly died because I remembered we had been fighting for so long and how the fuck are we supposed to raise a baby if we do nothing but row and I missed you so much and I'm really, really sorry and I don't want this to keep going on because it's just shit and we're supposed to be grown-ups and we are fucking crap. Please can we start again?'

And even in your relief at the end of hostilities, you know you're a bollox. You're a bollox because you don't have a baby in your belly. She was behaving oddly because of the demonic possession, you had no excuse bar the fact that you're a bollox and you were reacting out of some pitiful in-bred machismo. Not only that but your reaction was prolonged and, while at the start it may have been knee-jerk, you kept it going in a methodical manner to spite her and fight your sad little corner.

Yet, even with that realisation comes the glimmer that your fight was necessary. Because this is only the start. Your life as you knew it is gone; if you don't make some sort of a pathetic, retro Cro-Magnon stance everything that was dear to you will be discarded and you will be remoulded, jellymould style, into society's view of what a father should be. You don't know if you can take that.

But right now all you notice is that she's got quite a bit heavier, in a good way. You cup her waist and damn, suddenly she's got back. And bloody hell, would you check out these kegs. You can't believe you've wasted the last few weeks pouring poison down your neck with every long-lost mate you could dredge up to help fuel your escape when you could have been spending time with your head buried in these. The sex is magnificent in the way that sex with a lazy Irishman is magnificent. You both get off without leaving the couch and manage to avoid minor and major injuries that could be inflicted by the detritus lying around. Dinner is ordered via the phone, dispatched once again on the couch, the DVD is barely passable but acceptably so because you're both keen on taking to the pit for some more messy, make-up, newly kinky due to extra bulges, dirty shagging.

This is the window. Dive through it.

SCENARIO 2—FRANK

'I'm home!' you shout. You try to be enthusiastic when you come through the door, even though the announcement of your arrival is usually met with the type of disdain reserved for looters who have smashed into the house bent on pillage. You sometimes wonder would she rather see a posse of drug-fuelled gang rapists march towards her rather than your falsely enthusiastic face.

This time her voice comes from the kitchen. 'I've got the dinner going in here. Did you remember to pick up some basil?'

Shit. That's what you were supposed to get, not the latest copy of *Men's Health*. Dick. Here comes the pain.

'Oh, I'm sorry love, it went straight out of my head.' You arrive in the doorway prepared for whatever pot of bubbling sauce is to be thrown in your direction.

'Don't worry about it. I've bulked up on the rosemary, they mightn't have worked together anyway.' She looks up, 'How are you? How was work?'

Ooh, this is creepy. She had given up her own job six weeks earlier after attending a seminar that encouraged concentrated mother-baby bonding from conception. She had paid extra to spend some personal time with the facilitator after becoming terrified she may have damaged the baby by concentrating on financial futures instead of loving it in earnest for the first four weeks of its gestation. The baby expert (Eamon) had told her everything was fine but asked did she really see currency trading as the best way to forge a true, loving relationship with a son or daughter who would instinctively look to her for guidance in all matters, physical, spiritual and emotional, for the rest of their natural lives?

That was that. She didn't even see out her notice period, she simply refused to return to the office. Her boss, a cash-hungry ex-jock called Davis Patterson who lived up to the inanity of his name, was none too impressed but even he could see the black pregnancy mood descend and figured he was cutting his losses letting her go early. It put an end to any maternity payments and he assured her that there was a great chance her job would still be open should she choose to return after the child was born. You had learned of this only when you inquired why she wasn't rising for work with you that fateful Monday morning. When you heard what she had planned you didn't engage. Instead you went to work and ran the numbers. You're good at that.

They didn't add up.

Mortgage repayments, pension payments, two car loans and a trio of holidays abroad annually cost serious wedge. You earned marginally more than her but realistically what you were down to was a 50 per cent cut in income with a minimum one third addition to the household forthcoming. If you weren't scared shitless of both her and her miserable fuck of an old man you would have gone home and kicked her down the street back into the office.

Box clever, said the voice in your head. In the past six weeks you re-mortgaged to interest only, extended the duration of all loans, and cut pension and insurance payments back to the bone. You were still hitting the Visa for living expenses in the last week of the month. Why she had to start buying organic baby clothes from earthmother.com at this stage you could not fathom, but dared not question.

You put on a brave face, told friends and family that in order for both mother and baby to maximise the benefits of pregnancy they had come to a mutual agreement that she should leave work. To reduce stress, you see. Hers obviously. It would involve some tightening of the belt, but nothing you couldn't manage, you're doing well enough. Nothing to worry about really. Oh fuuucccccckkkkkk, everything was going to shit.

Now here you are, clutching a fitness magazine you can't afford and expecting to wear some pasta sauce after another sixty-hour work week.

'Why don't you uncork that bottle of Chablis your mother brought over last time. I think I can stretch to a glass tonight. The baby seems to fancy one, she's been very kind to me today.'

She always called the baby 'she'. You're praying for a boy, more to piss her off than anything. You don't care what it is, but had found yourself referring to it as 'he' on occasion. And then paying for it later.

'I rang Davis today. Told him I wanted my job back part-time, that I'd been slightly unhinged when I decided to quit, the baby and all that shit. So, I'm in from next week, Tuesday to Thursday with full maternity benefits restored. What do you think about that then?' She's looking at you rather cheekily with the wine glass at her lips.

'What brought that on? I thought Eamon [the baby guru, an ex-dairy farmer from West Cork who now drives a new 7-series] was dead set against working through pregnancy, that it might upset the negative ions in the womb. Or something like that.'

'Well, I had a flick through some credit card and bank statements that you conveniently left sitting on the hall table and realised we were in the shit. To be honest I've been bored off my tits watching box-sets of *Friends* here during the day and fancy getting back to work while I can. I knew Davis would be a pussy about it so I told him to shut the fuck up when he started to complain. Eamon was a bit more of a problem, but he's a fucking hippy charlatan with his heart set on a villa in Tuscany. Even so, I'm only going back three days, full-time would be too much of a strain for my little girl wonder.'

At this she pats her belly knowingly. You resist the urge to crumple with relief, swallow your glass down in one and pour another.

'Now,' she says, 'You get your arse up those stairs. We haven't been shagging half enough these days and that sauce needs to simmer.'

This is the window. Dive through it.

THE THIRD TRIMESTER: CALL THE EXORCIST

It is noticeable in the last section on the second trimester that there was no mention of gestation developments. There is a simple reason for this: why disturb a good thing with science? When things are tricky, science can help explain the facts. When they're good, adopt the hippy mantra and increase the peace, bro, go with the flow, you don't need to know what's happening in there. One thing is sure and obvious; she's getting bigger from months three to six, bigger and better some might say. Unfortunately, around six months there is a tipping point, the point where the fun in being big stops for Mum, when she realises she's quite big enough and yet only set to get bigger. And when the fun stops for Mum, the fun stops for you. Welcome to Trimester Three.

We're blokes, we're not simpletons, we are aware of the ultimate goal of pregnancy. That at the end of what has seemed an interminable tunnel there is a smaller tunnel from which will be emitted an object of a size that has no right to fit through. That object will, in turn, dictate the course of the rest of your life, but for now we have to bring our focus to getting it out.

In our house the book that became the pregnancy bible was *The New Pregnancy and Childbirth* by Sheila Kitzinger (Penguin 1997 [though this was a battered second-hand copy and I'm sure they've updated it to include extra-bloody colour photos by now]). A work colleague brought it into the office one day and proffered it as a gift. I started to browse and was immediately accosted by black and white graphic images of birth. The book went into my bag, was handed to the mother on my return home that day and over the following months I occasionally sneaked peeks on days I felt particularly strong. But it was only after the birth that the true understatement of the language used about pregnancy came home to me. If history books were written in the style of pregnancy books we would refer to the skirmish that occurred between 1939 and 1945 involving an aggressive little man with a moustache and a possible messiah complex. The English would be said to have 'visited' Ireland for seven hundred years and the Vietnam war remembered as a joyous American attempt to nudge the natives away from the path of communism.

Here is one of my favourite passages from *The New Pregnancy* on the topic of 'The last few weeks':

> *Conflicting emotions are characteristic of these last weeks. You may be tired of being pregnant, but on the other hand the state you are now in is a condition you know and understand, whereas in front of you there is an unknown challenge ... Some women say that as the birth day draws nearer they feel irritated with the pregnancy.*

If conflicting emotions involve varying from minor psychotic tendencies to full-on homicidal mania, then that first sentence is an accurate representation. The 'state you are now in' may be familiar to women at this stage but there don't seem too many who wouldn't be willing to sell a kidney to get into any other state at this stage of developments.

As for the possibility that the mother might 'feel irritated', let it be known that when you enter a house containing a woman in the latter stages of pregnancy you are walking into a lion's den where the she-lion has not eaten in three weeks and has just had her cubs slaughtered in front of her. To top it all, you are wearing *eau d'antelope* and nothing else.

This is not the time to revert to the behaviour of the first trimester and hang it all and lash into the gargle. Now is a time to attempt to show some backbone, to offer comfort, to be resilient, to rub swollen feet, offer assurances of continuing beauty and deny the existence of varicose veins. You don't do this for selfish reasons, thinking that these brownie points may be stored away and cashed in later on. There is no hope of that. You do this for basic survival.

The New Pregnancy also briefly mentions something called

'antenatal depression' which:

> *though usually shortlived and spasmodic is a fact of life for some women. It may suggest a need for more rest. You may feel very different if you lie down to rest in a darkened room in the middle of the day, have some early nights and adjust your activity to slower, gentler rhythms if possible.*

You may have come to terms with seeing your exotic, sexy, vibrant young lover transform into a sweaty, heaving, tracksuited manatee over the course of these last few weeks, but you might be struggling with her never moving off her arse and forever barking orders from the couch where she sits for twelve hours a day, whenever possible, eating Ritz crackers smeared with Philadelphia and onions. When she tells you she's depressed and needs to lie down more to adjust her activity to slower, gentler rhythms you must resist the urge to guffaw in disbelief that an animal that has personally developed a turning circle similar in ratio to a small planet could possibly move any slower. Remember, you love her and your kid is responsible for this.

You may have some inclination that she could be milking the situation. Again, keep this thought to yourself. Practise the art, no matter how difficult it is to comprehend, of thinking things without speaking them out loud. Maybe some women do fake the difficulty of the latter stages of pregnancy, but who are we to suggest such a thing? What is achingly apparent is that this is an uncomfortable period for Mum, a discomfort not aided by the knowledge that it will only be ended by experiencing a pain all women wave in our faces as the ultimate in agony. Our tales of kicks in the nuts, dislocated shoulders and root canal treatment are pooh-poohed as mere itches to be scratched in comparison to the trial of bringing life into the world.

They are, of course, right. So be nice in T3; they have a shit time coming.

Chapter 3
Birth

PREPARE FOR THE HORROR IN ITS ENTIRETY

My dad wasn't at my birth and that was fine. In the early seventies if the father had insisted on being present in the delivery ward he would have been looked on as an oddity, by his wife (of course they would have been married) and the medical staff. But back then there would have been a doctor present so he would have had little need for concern. Now you have as much chance of the janitor delivering your baby as of a consultant being involved.

You may or may not have attended ante-natal classes with Mum. If you have to go to these things, do so with a light heart, as you're probably getting free time from work. Bring a good book or an iPod because the chances are, even if you absorb everything that's being taught, it'll all go out the window when the screaming starts. These classes operate on the presumption that you can be some use in the delivery ward. You can't. You may have to stand in for a midwife on occasion as she rushes from bed to bed attempting to deliver three children at once because the government neglected to employ staff in the previous twelve months, but then it may be better if you're not there and the midwife is forced to stay.

These classes are made up of varying numbers of first-time parents. For some unknown reason, despite the fact that everyone is there with a common purpose, nobody speaks to anyone else. An experienced practitioner will take ten hour-long sessions to demonstrate breathing techniques, squatting positions, useful massage exercises and finally come to the drugs that are available. One in every ten couples will announce that they're intending on having a natural childbirth, sit back and smile smugly. They will then sentence themselves to confusion and consternation as Mum begs for pain relief during the event and regrets not taking in her options.

The rest will perk up and listen to the information they came for in the first place. There is a reason anaesthesia was invented, and it was quite likely to ease the distress of squeezing out a watermelon. In any event, the exhortations of the class leader for the dad to administer iced water and whisper words of encouragement during labour are about as useful as encouraging a jumper to relax, as he leaps from the top of the Empire State Building.

In Sydney there has been a development in the ante-natal class regime. Rather than the stale, antiseptic atmosphere of a hospital room, one couple decided to offer an alternative in their local pub. Fuelled by schooners of Victoria Bitter the men are more inclined to engage with the questions that have been plaguing them but they have been uncomfortable about asking. These have included addressing the possible presence of the mother-in-law in the delivery ward as requested by Mum. Is this just awkward or is it actually emasculating? Another Bruce shared how he had left the hospital to change his clothes during labour. On his way home he realised his car was too small to cope with the demands of his family now that the third child was being born and so made a detour to a dealership. He arrived back to the hospital with forms in hand and managed to stall the birth as he had his Sheila sign them between contractions.

While the war stories flowed freely with the booze, the chances are that it makes little difference to the actual event. It is undoubtedly a good reason to get out to the boozer and 'do something together' as you've probably been hounded to do. Attend these classes to maintain harmony during pregnancy if that works for you. Do not expect to learn anything practical.

For some reason, in the late seventies dads were for the first time encouraged to be present in delivery wards. Through the eighties and nineties this encouragement developed into insistence. For you to suggest now that you would rather be elsewhere while this gut-splitting procedure unfolds is akin to admitting a predilection for boiling puppies in hot oil or, even worse, driving a large, petrol-powered SUV. It might be the greatest victory of feminism that men are now expected to share in the pain of childbirth where before our predecessors sipped Scotch, smoked Players and 'waited for news'.

Our other source of childbirth information has always been TV and films. For years I sat and watched babies being delivered on soap operas with a couple of grunts, a modicum of resentment and a soupçon of effort. My mother would sit on the couch and mutter disdainfully as the baby made its first appearance, 'There's a lovely six-week-old babba.' I never understood why she got so worked up by the depiction of unfolding events. Now I do. The real story does not involve the sassy mother squeezing the father's hand so hard she breaks a finger during the thirty seconds of her delivery, rather it features the eighteen hours she endured interminable agony in real life and insisted the other party be present for every moment of it.

There are two things that every new father should be made aware of before entering the birthing arena, and none of the official avenues prepare you for this so listen up close. You have known the woman who is about to give birth to your child for a minimum of nine months, probably a while longer. You have seen her at her best and her worst. You have both loved her and possibly desired her execution. You have seen her grow, figuratively and physically. You think you know her. You think you know all of her. But get ready, because you're about to get to know all of her in ways you couldn't have imagined. Or if you have, you spend time on websites you would rather your wife and the general populace never learn about.

The two words they don't mention in the ante-natal classes are 'blood' and 'shit'. Every day midwives and nurses head off to their jobs and we look at them and think how wonderful it must be to spend your working day (or night) embracing new life. What they really do every day is dive into the abyss, to wade through troughs of blood and shit. At the end of each bout they are involved in, they are presented with another blood- and shit-soaked little person. To us, the parents, that screaming, slimy, gasping creature embodies all our emotions, hopes and visions of the future. The wonder of midwives is that they make each birth feel incredible when, in physical terms, it can only be a daily struggle through the drama of entering the world, a drama that is each time a huge physical effort for child and mother. Into which is thrown a useless father that takes up space in a room he has no business being in.

But at least midwives and nurses are experienced in the regular explosions of bodily fluids that accompany each of our arrivals. At least the mother, while bearing the brunt of the events herself, is so caught up in her own situation that she is unaware of the carnage between her legs. The only person in the room who has had no preparation for this Somme-like scene, and without a physical distraction, is you. And you are expected to remain supportive, encouraging and meditative throughout. All the while you are pushed from pillar to post by nurse, midwife and matron as they take it in turns to either disappear as Mum appears about to die, or line up to insert various lengths of arm into the part of your partner that until now you thought only you got to play with. For the first time, the realisation that you won't be treating that spot as your personal funfair for a while raises its head. And having seen the exploded cauliflower it has become, you breathe a sigh of relief.

Due to either staff shortages or a misguided attempt to include you in events, the midwife may request that you hold various legs up or down, your partner up or down, wipe away bits that have fallen off or out of her, try not to slip in the puddles that have formed around her and all the while retain a gentle and positive demeanour.

We are not trained for this. We have not evolved to have any part in this. No other male animal is present at the birth of his child, and yet we are expected to be delighted to have the opportunity presented to us, usually by childless spinsters, to witness the miracle of birth. Clichéd as it is, the miracle is that anybody does it a second time.

So, for all these misgivings, the sad fact is that we have to accept we will be dragged in and we are expected to smile while doing it.

If any guidance can be offered, maybe the following will help:

Don't go near the hospital until you are absolutely sure she is in labour (more about this particular bugbear in the next section).

Try to have rested well in advance. A useful tip is to hit the bed the first time she says she needs to go to the hospital because in reality you're probably about eight to twelve hours away from needing to move.

Bring some grub and eat it before things get messy.

Get ready for a long bout of caterwauling.

Offer to go out to the shop for anything anyone wants, anyone in the delivery room, the ward itself, out in the corridor, in the hospital in general. Anything that gets you outside where you can take up smoking again and swallow some Valium without any rolling of eyes.

Encourage all family members to turn up. If she tires of your trembling and contortions she may take pity on you and ask that you tag somebody else, someone who actually has balls (in her words), as a replacement.

Try to get your head around the fact that your mind will be blown by the act and your heart will burst at the arrival.

THE BROTHERHOOD OF FATHERHOOD

To state the obvious, the delivery ward is life and occasionally death, yet many of us fellas approach it with an attitude bordering on the blasé because we have been given to understand that what will happen is a straightforward, natural procedure. If anything in this life has cemented my firm belief that if there is a God it is a cruel, uncaring one, it is childbirth. Nothing natural should be this hard. Nothing this hard should be witnessed by another human being, especially someone who has designs on sleeping with the person involved ever again. To support us through this trying time we need to support one another and affirm the brotherhood of fatherhood.

Okay, among the horror stories there are the occasional tales of envy-inducing ease: the equivalent of the Catholic mother in Monty Python's *The Meaning of Life* dropping sprogs with liquid fluidity. These women exist. They arrive home (if they haven't already delivered there while wallpapering the nursery) a day later and start cooking a five-course meal for thirty friends and family. Her child hangs suckling at her breast as if he had always been there, and may never leave. These women in the past were martyrs, suffragettes, politicos, women for whom suffering was as expected as it was ordinary and destined to failure. These women feel no pain.

Their men, however, deserve our wrath. They weaken the brotherhood. They sit back and wonder at everyone else's post-traumatic stress disorder, occasionally disregarding what happens as nonsense. These men are to be watched and should not be allowed the freedom to undermine what has been a collectively harrowing time for the majority of our brothers. It is them, with their smug 'isn't it all just a great big larf' heads that do our role in the birth process the greatest disservice. As they lounge around guffawing that their wonder seed leads to miracle births we should avail of any opportunity to cut them down to size and make them suffer as we will or already have. The ultimate glory would be to somehow manoeuvre your own unavailability on birthing day and have such a Wonder Seed Dad go in your place.

For this is no laughing matter. You must be mentally strong to deal with the delivery ward, to witness your partner being skewered and gutted to exit your creation from her body, to be a proactive part of the team. Anyone that undermines your role has either never witnessed a birth, is a Wonder Seed Dad, or a woman. The first and the last can be excused, but another man should never diminish the brotherhood of fatherhood. At a time when we need to stand together, no-one should stand to the side smirking. We have enough people undermining our role in this without betrayal from within. Remember the brotherhood.

IS SHE REALLY IN LABOUR, OR IS SHE JUST FOOLING AROUND?

Here is the curse of the first-time father. You want this to go well for you and her. You want it to be like the movies, for her waters to break while you're standing in the kitchen arguing over an inconsequential thing. You'll look at each other and realise what's important in life, grab the bag that's waiting at the door and speed to the hospital. There, you know, she will have a tough time and you will bumble around, using humour to dispel all problems until finally, with a great big heave, she will discharge your heir into your arms. The whole thing will pass in a matter of hours. You will kiss your woman's forehead gently before taking the swaddled child out to the waiting room where three generations of both families will have patched up long-running feuds and greet you with a raucous cheer before your father-in-law pops a Cuban in your gob and finally forgives you for knocking up his angel in the first place.

You've played out the scenario in your head many times, and who knows, it may turn out like that. But the first myth to dispel is the procedure starting quickly. Occasionally it happens as described above, but usually you find yourself diving for the door each time she has a burst of indigestion or a slight cramp. Keep this up and you could be itching at the starting line for weeks so when the action kicks off, your resources are depleted and you wander, finally, into the delivery room a shell of a man.

It's B-Day. She hasn't gone early and you've marked every day off the calendar and reached the one marked with a red ring. The only difference is she is still lugging around an extra forty pounds but now has to field constant phone calls inquiring after developments. Go to the office, the building site, the garden, wherever you go and presume nothing will happen until her doctor says he'll have to induce her if proceedings do not commence within forty-eight hours. Sleep, eat, don't drink too much no matter how much you want to, and wait for nature to rouse from its slumber and take its course.

Most importantly, don't hotfoot it to the hospital every time she farts. Maternity hospitals are full of expectant first-time parents sitting, sweating, sure the baby is on its way when the urchin has probably just stretched its legs mid-nap with no intention of leaving its scratcher for days yet. At this point, with both of you on tenterhooks, the last place you need to be is within earshot of screaming mothers in the throes of labour. She thinks she's in pain, you think you're coping really well, you hear one prolonged, agonised yawp from down the hall and realise you haven't entered the realm of possibilities. You want to be somewhere else until it really is your turn. Finally an over-worked midwife will cast a cold eye in your shivering direction, shove her arm in Mum up to her elbow, pronounce that she hasn't started dilating yet and tell you both to feck off home and stop wasting everyone's time. This is not good for morale and should be avoided.

Anxiety is prone to running riot once B-Day has passed. Mum is as big as she is ever going to be, she can't turn full-circle without applying for a visa from adjoining countries, and in her mind's eye she had seen herself sipping her first glass of champagne in months while throngs of friends and family gather round her bed to admire the most beautiful child ever born. This has not happened, instead she faces into the uncharted waters of late delivery with nothing but her varicose veins and Nobby Stiles for company. It is, of course, your fault.

You can buy into this rising fervour or you can continue on about your daily business. Nothing has changed until baby makes an appearance. The doctor gave you a date and that date is gone. Make supportive noises, do whatever is asked of you, do not in any way suggest that you have been put out too, and subtly try to encourage baby out without displaying your impatience. This requires nuance of movement, something prospective fathers are not noted for. But, most of all, do not vacate the comfort of your own home for the clinical lights of the hospital until you are sure it is time, no matter how much she demands to be shifted.

As a man, you will be disregarded in all things internal. Employ a team of mothers to come in and discuss the lengths of their respective labours, to supplicate her with encouraging stories about how the pain she is feeling now is merely a warm-up for the agony ahead. Instil a sense of pride in holding out for as long as possible at home without moving. As a rule of thumb, if you can't see a head between her legs she's still just feeling the effects of that red curry she had two days before.

If, however, baby is actually being stubborn and the notion of inducement or Caesarean section has been raised, you want to start proactively getting on the case. There are a number of avenues available to you, some more pleasurable than others:

Walk. It makes sense, there's gravitational pressure on baby and swaying hips might free him up.

Sex. All the pregnancy websites and magazines suggest that the woman might have difficulty feeling sexy at this late stage but if she can muster the energy for a late ride it could have movement-inducing consequences. What they don't mention is how the father is expected to rise to the occasion when faced with a raging, bulbous partner shouting at him to 'Just get stuck in and do the business you impotent ponce!' You should bear in mind that this final act of love may have the added benefit of returning your partner to her body in place of Kathy Bates's character from *Misery* who seems to have possessed it. Take one for the team lads.

Castor oil. This is a real old wives' classic. The recommendation is to swig down one to four ounces of castor oil mixed with six ounces of orange juice to negate the oiliness. Castor oil will empty your bowels in a couple of hours and the logic is that soon after, everything else will fall out too. If she'll swallow this, you should have no trouble getting her to swallow anything. Park that one for later.

Spicy food. Some people swear that it was the vindaloo wot done it, guv. Seems a bit fishy, even if it was supposed to be lamb, to me. Chances are if she hits labour with a bellyful of chillies, she's going to have to spraypaint the walls in the not too distant future. Chances are that you'll be directly in the path of the required wall. Tread this path if you're hungry. Or constipated.

Blue and black cohosh. This is a herbal treatment. Blue cohosh is believed to make uterine contractions stronger, while black cohosh may regulate the contractions. Together, they work to make contractions more effective. As with most herbal remedies, there is absolutely no evidence that this works but it might buy you some time before she expects you to have sex again.

Nipple stimulation. Nice. Rubbing the old raspberry ripples can bring about the release of oxytocin which can cause contractions which, in turn, can evolve into labour. This is not hugely popular as a means of inducing labour among medical practitioners as it can lead to excessively long, strong uterine contractions sometimes resulting in fetal heart rate slowing. So, you either do this under supervision, which sounds a little pervy, or not at all.

Massage. You can choose to rub the rabid, beached whale yourself or get a trained massage therapist in to stimulate trigger points for labour. The idea is that when stress is reduced her body might chill and push out a totally relaxed little blighter.

Booze. Again, not a great body of evidence to suggest that this works but it just might calm Mum down. Stop her after the first bottle though, or she'll be all over the sex option again.

Right, presuming one of those works, it's about time you got yourself into hospital and started on the real work.

PAIN RELIEF AND HOW TO CONVINCE HER TO USE IT

Cast your mind back to those ante-natal classes you were forced to attend. At some point the midwife in charge would have outlined the pain relief available to a mother in labour. Most mothers in the developed world have the good sense to take whatever they can get but there are a few who believe that the birth of a child is the most natural thing in the world and should be completed unaided, as her mother and grandmother before her did it. Such is the single-mindedness of this type of mother that she will then disregard her own mother as she attempts to explain how she would have chewed through her own leg to get to an epidural if only one had been available.

There is a growing band of mothers who receive a lot of negative press, those who opt for the elective Caesarean. The so-called 'too posh to push' brigade are then pilloried further for daring to have cosmetic surgery done while they are under anaesthetic to remove their jelly bellies. This synergy of procedures appears to me to be the conjoinment of the best of both worlds. Mum accepts that she is putting herself at unnecessary risk but is determined to avoid the pain of delivery and will be returned to you a tightened and somewhat retuned model. You escape the delivery ward saga. Obviously this is a vain path to tread and possibly a waste of hospital resources, but it is the woman's prerogative.

Much more dangerous is the holistic, hopeful Mum. No matter what, she's seeing this through on nothing but happy hormones and you're coming with her. She'll have her homeopathy kit at the ready and a determined glint in her eye. She'll remind you that she hasn't taken a Nurofen for a hangover in years and she can cope with this.

Your job here is to assure her that when the need arises, grabbing the anaesthetist by the throat and demanding that he plug her full of morphine will not be remembered as an act of weakness or ever referred to as a failure. If, when the time comes, you can convince him to give you a jab on the sly, so much the better.

EXCUSES FOR AVOIDING THE DELIVERY WARD

As discussed earlier, being present for the birth of your child is now seen as an obligation rather than an option. Having come this far, you are committed to being present from start to finish. So, be very careful about choosing to slip away when the shit literally starts to hit the fan.

Labour takes hours, sometimes days. If an epidural has been administered and is effective the only sign that contractions are taking place will be increased blips on the bedside monitor every few minutes. If she is fighting them on her own terms, however, every contraction will be like stepping into a ring for a minute at a time with George Foreman in his prime. She won't find them easy either. Your job is to soothe through each one and accept personal responsibility for every dagger-like skewer of agony she experiences. You cannot stand up and walk away, but you can make yourself available to every request she has. If she needs extra support, hunt out pillows throughout the building. If she needs cooling down, check every tap in the place until you find the coolest one and visit the kitchen with precise instructions for ice-making. If she is hot, hunt down a fan, visit Argos to buy one, contact an air-conditioning contractor and negotiate rates for installation.

Make yourself busy. This is a map for fatherhood in itself. At all times appear busy and involved in what's going on, but allow yourself to be dragged away to attend to management issues beyond the actual scene. Each time you return with your mission accomplished you have marked up another success to be recorded for later confirmation and also killed valuable, screaming labour time.

Worried at the pain she is enduring, seek out a consultant with the intention of demanding that her situation be monitored. Your quest will make Frodo's destruction of a ring seem like a stroll to the corner shop for a litre of low fat milk and will probably result in your playing eighteen holes at an exclusive country club in a neighbouring county. By the time you have an actual doctor examine her, she will be nearing delivery. At which point you should tell anybody with MD after their name to vacate the premises and let the people who have some idea what's going on, i.e. midwife and nurses, get on with their jobs.

ARRIVAL AND BEING A HERO

What you don't want to do is miss the birth. If, after all your running around, you arrive to Mum holding baby by herself you will have missed an event so important to both her and the child you will never be able to begin to kiss enough ass to reassume any level of parity in your relationship again. It is essential that you are there for the endgame.

If you have been organised in preparation for baby's arrival you should already have purchased a baby monitor for use at home. A good idea is to bring this into the hospital. During a particularly chaotic moment, place the listening end somewhere discreetly in the delivery ward and keep the receiver in your own pocket. As you roam on your many errands, listen in regularly to assess how close to popping point things are. Once you hear the magic words 'Ten centimetres dilated', get yourself back there. If you miss that line and you tune into someone shouting 'Push, push, push, push!' you need to hurry. Don't forget to remove the listening device when your session is over or you could be accused of all sorts of dodgy misdemeanours when the next mother takes her place in the room. Justifying a minor fetish for the aural experience of childbirth should not be high on the your list of priorities in your first few days with new baby.

You can be pretty sure that when Mum gets the nod to start pushing she's going to look around for you. If you're not there, despite her current situation, the blind fury will rise and she will begin consciously or unconsciously to plot reducing the rest of your time on this planet to a living hell. Entering the last furlong, this is not a good frame of mind for mother or baby. Ensuring that you arrive before these murderous thoughts take hold could well result in her relief being so great that you may forever appear the great saviour. This is unlikely, but it's an idea worth clinging to. There are few moments in life where we can even half-heartedly aspire to heroism, it's wise to grasp each one when they arise.

But leaving aside all wish-fulfilment for a moment, there are few truer experiences than being present at a birth. On an evolutionary scale we appear to have moved on from our ancestors struggling to spark a flame for heat, but to witness birth is to become part of a line of humanity stretching back through time. There is intense struggle, there is pain, there is danger, and finally there is life. It is easy to explain the biological process, much more difficult to get any grasp on the emotional. To witness a woman in the throes of labour, bringing all her power to bear on releasing the child from her care, is to witness an animal in its basest form with all pretence stripped aside. She is doing a job that her body was designed for. But this does not explain the male response, the desire to protect and encourage that rushes through every part of you. Nor does it begin to explain the overwhelming rush of connection to that woman and wondrous love for your child when finally he or she arrives spluttering and mewling into the world. For when that happens you really are a hero, and, more importantly, so is Mum, and most of all, so is baby.

This event takes place every minute of every day around the world, and for every person involved it is one of the great moments in their lives. It could be made to appear commonplace; it is not. It is huge. Be there and breathe it in.

MEETING YOUR HEIR

While my missus was pregnant with our first child I drove the country in a daze. I was in an office job that required me to travel a little, but for that period I took full advantage of my freedom and hit the road relentlessly. I didn't accomplish any more work because that wasn't the motivating factor. I drove to daydream and listen to music.

Much of my fantasies revolved around music. I imagined driving my son or daughter to school and them getting involved in singing along to songs I liked. They would think I was so suave, Rico Suavé. I imagined the big discussions with them: sex, drugs, relationships, problems with their mother, school, career. In all these situations I was the voice of reason, bringing my considerable experience to bear, for which they would be hugely grateful. They would spend their days grooving to the Happy Mondays and coming to their dad for advice. They were rosy, those fantasies of mine.

At the time I had little or no exposure to small children. I had a couple of nieces, but they lived far away and when we went to visit they had no interest in watching football on telly so we rarely had much to say to each other. Occasionally colleagues would bring their children into the office and I would watch female staff members gather in clusters and coo. Fathers would hang back but be comfortable when drawn in for comment, while the single geezers would suddenly find something urgent to take care of and slip out the back door for cigarettes. I should at the time have paid more attention to the correlation between children and the need for cigarettes.

I should also have paid more attention to the details of my daydreams for none of them involved a creature without the power to speak, sit up or tell you what was wrong with it. In each one, our living space was clean and harmonious and there was no evidence of having to clean up anyone's bodily excretions. In short, I had no concept of a baby, what one would want or need. What one was. The few I had met were at least washed and powdered, nothing had prepared me for the ball of blood, shit and mucous that was to come thundering from between my girlfriend's thighs when finally she decided to grant us an appearance. Yet that meeting was, without doubt, the most important meeting of my life to that point.

My father had phoned in the previous couple of weeks. He admits himself he has no interest in babies, he would rather you took them away until they reach at least seven months when they begin to attempt to communicate. Until that point I don't recall him ever making reference to us as babies, apart from the day my sister was born and she marked her arrival by urinating straight down his tie as he inspected her for the first time. He wears that story like a badge of honour. The day he rang he warned me to try and prepare for being overwhelmed. I remember hearing his words but having no understanding of what he meant.

The morning I sat with my finger clasped by my daughter through the opening of an incubator I got it. The earth had shifted on its axis ever so slightly. I couldn't speak without my voice becoming caught in my throat, I couldn't think what to do next. It didn't matter what I would do next because I was content to sit and have my finger held forever. Her mother lay exhausted in her bed, grimly content, watching us and I was aware that she was watching me as much as her new child. Simply because I could not get to grips with the way I was feeling—in awe of the mother, in thrall to the daughter. Alternating between gasping down huge sobs of relief and jigging on the spot, I had no idea what was to come next. As long as she continued to hold that finger.

We had arrived at that point after a long, haphazard weekend, having been sent home from the hospital twice to wait until it was worth coming in. When finally admitted, after two days spent nursing her aching belly in the bath tub, the missus announced her birth plan to her midwife—no pain relief to be administered and could her mother be present as well as me, the father, to supply homeopathic remedies when necessary.

Through the course of a protracted and agonising eleven-hour labour she wound up swallowing every piece of pain relief the medical system had to offer. This started when she was given oxytocin to 'improve the efficiency of her contractions', according to the nurse. She also mentioned that the pain of the contractions may increase somewhat. Within half an hour the missus was writhing like a demented banshee, eyes rolling in her head like a mad cow, staring straight through me and speaking gibberish to an unseen presence in the room.

She accepted gas and air first. It was like applying a Band-Aid to first-degree burns. Pethadine followed, but this merely intensified her delirium. After ten hours the midwife examined her again, announced that there had been little development and said that this was the last opportunity she would have to opt for an epidural. They would soon have to start thinking about a section. She looked at the missus and asked, 'Do you want to have an anaesthetist administer an epidural? I need you to ask for one yourself.'

The missus was lying slumped to her left side, her arm and head hanging off the edge of the bed. She looked up at the midwife and furrowed her brow, seemingly confused at the question. She lay there and stared.

I knelt beside her. 'Do you want to take something to stop the pain? It's okay if you do, it will make things easier.'

She turned her confused look at me and whispered, 'Yeah.'

'You have to say it to the nurse.'

She peered vaguely into the room, muttering in her exhaustion, 'Yes, I do.'

Immediately the midwife turned on her heel to find someone to do the job. The missus told me afterwards that, as she had been asked the question, she felt she had been staring at the midwife and in her head was screaming, 'Of course I do you stupid bitch. Look at the state of me, I'm fucked! Give me the drugs or I'll fucking die, just give them to me now!' In her depleted state she had no idea that her rantings were purely personal, oblivious to anyone without a hotline to her brain.

A half hour later a needle had been inserted into her spine and magic juice fed into her system. Minutes later she was sitting up looking around as if she had just arrived in the room. The contractions raged on, judging by the whittering of the bedside machine, but she was no more concerned with them than she was with the Northern Irish peace process right then.

The midwife returned and did her by now familiar disappearing arm routine. She estimated a couple of hours to go and told me to slip off to the waiting room and get some kip. I laughed at the possibility of going AWOL and the missus smiled and told me to get lost; calm and somewhat high she fancied a chat with her mum before the main event. I left them nattering comfortably where only an hour before it seemed Wes Craven was filming a feature. Ten minutes later I was asleep on a hard floor. I have never witnessed a more surreal turnabout.

In our anxiety we had made every first-time parent wrong turn. Days later it seemed like we were getting somewhere.

I was woken for the big push. It took an hour. She brought every ounce of rejuvenated energy she had stored in her drugged recovery to bear and heaved that creature out. It was a display of such intense courage that I could only wonder where she found the will. I never expected to witness anything quite so single-minded again until she exceeded herself three years later to squeeze out the younger child in another protracted and difficult birth. In both cases what was most striking was the drama, the heightened tension, the result, the relief, and then our awareness of another. As quiet descends a new person makes their presence felt and announces their arrival. The hero has entered the story.

My experience of meeting both my children was to be washed with a wave of love. Nothing prepared me for being hit so hard with a simple need to hold and protect this person or for the sense of being linked irrevocably to another human being. It would seem obvious that a mother would feel this, having until recently had this person as part of her own physicality, but it seems the male experience is very similar, despite only being there at the very start and the very end. Many other fathers have spoken of this initial recognition of something of their own, an acknowledgement of part of themselves being contained in this new body, a feeling of responsibility and a gratitude for that. It hits like a brick to the head. It puts every heart-wrenching teenage crush and subsequent rejection in the shade. It is a pure connection and an oasis of relevance in a world of inconsequentialities. The pity is that this purity has to ever be sullied by your and the child's own imperfections because if you could bottle that moment there's a slight chance you could make a few quid.

Some fathers don't experience this. Some witness a birth as a physical act that does not pull at their perception of the world but merely represents the delivery of another one of us. When I first heard a father speak of this I felt sorry for him. Then he continued to explain how he was slowly getting to know that child, finishing with the line, 'I think I can love her.' It seemed like a slow-burning version of the lightning flash I and many others were hammered with in the delivery room. It sounded more analytical but at the same time more grounded than the alternative love bomb. Either way, it seems that we all come to a similar realisation: that this is for keeps. One way is to launch head first into the deep end, while the other is to walk slowly into the shallows. Sooner or later you're swimming, and you have a baby on your back.

She continued to hold my finger while inserting half of her other hand into her mouth and sucking insistently. It was early morning and the blinds were pulled. Sunlight angled into the ward while her mother slept and I gazed on the baby, thinking of a future that was no longer my own. Dust danced in the air and for the first time the hospital was quiet, as if an order had been given for the moment to be noticed. She held my finger and I held my head.

Chapter 4

Baby Comes Home— The First Month

YOU DON'T LIVE HERE ANY MORE
Remember your gaff? The one you spent the last few years getting right. Forget about it, it's not yours any more. Getting it right might mean you finally got round to stacking your collection of *Loaded* magazines in chronological order or it could mean you just invested fifty grand in an integrated Bang & Olufsen sound system, but either way it doesn't matter. All that matters now is that you never run out of nappies.

YOUR WOMAN IS A FOODBAG
There are many irritating aspects to pregnancy and birth. Chief among these is the wow factor among women. The actual act of giving birth is truly awe-inspiring to witness, and it leaves you wondering at the necessity of it being so difficult. Is it so that we won't overrun the world? Is it to remind us that the parcel, when it arrives, is a huge responsibility? These are big themes, they deserve attention, and they deserve a wow when any breakthrough or insight is revealed. It's all the other wows that undermine the big wows.

Misuse of language has a lot to do with this. Woman gets pregnant and oftentimes she and her posse of friends lose their powers of reason. One of the key topics of discussion during the nine months is the never-ending discussion about the gender of the child.

'What do you think it's going to be? Boy or a girl?'

Standard male reply: 'As far as I can see, chances are it'll be a boy or a girl. There don't seem to be any other options.'

'Come on,' says random girl involved, 'Don't be a killjoy, boy or girl?'

This conversation can't go any further. Off the top of our heads we can't identify the sex. Yet the topic can be stretched to include pontification on the size and shape of the bump, food gestation, brothers, sisters, cousins, how the mother feels when petting a dog, whether she's horny in the evenings or not and all manner of nonsense. Get a scan and have a professional tell you; end the musings.

Next up is the beauty of the mother. Throughout pregnancy Mum has to be assured at all times she is ravishing. Despite the fact that she has put on five stone and can't keep her face out of a bucket of KFC she must be continually informed that she is glowing and her inner gorgeousness is shining through. This is all good, positive encouragement and doesn't need to be undermined. Often, in fact, it is true and a pregnant mum can achieve a kind of luminescence she never had before. Sometimes, though, it is a stretch and we all know it.

The truth is abused most of all when Mum comes home with baby. This is a momentous occasion, the point to which all the planning, weeping and gnashing of teeth of the previous nine months has been building up. The house has been prepared, friends, neighbours and work colleagues, for the first child anyway, make themselves available and everybody takes their first teetering steps into a new world together. Mum is at her weakest. She has laid her egg and is facing into the unknown, realising that she knows as much about raising a child as she does about the off-side rule. All her sensitive female friends will pull together and comment on how well she looks. You will wonder how come she's still so fat and is there a possibility she could shower.

The fact is, whether she has chosen to breastfeed or not, at the outset she is a bag of food. And she looks it.

Another fact is that whether she has chosen to breastfeed or not, you most certainly are not in a position to comment. The prevailing attitude to breastfeeding among healthcare professionals is that it is to be encouraged, but this is in direct contrast to the advice doled out back in the seventies and eighties. Who is to say there won't be a similar turnaround in years to come? In the face of overwhelming pressure to breastfeed, some mothers feel a deep guilt at choosing to use a bottle. This is unfair on them and the child as, nutritionally, modern formula milk provides almost all the goodness of natural 'draught'. Even mothers who choose to feed often struggle with the practicalities of it.

But breastfeeding is free, convenient and natural. If it goes smoothly Mum's happy, baby's chuffed and you, my friend, are on easy street for however long you can convince her to keep going. As a rule of thumb, once the nipper can ask for a drop himself, then it's probably time to stop.

Some of the benefits of breastfeeding include the kid having less chance of suffering ear infections, diarrhoea and respiratory illness. It might also reduce the risk of breast and ovarian cancers[1] and can help in the development of a bond between mother and child. These are good things for all concerned, but you might be struggling with coming to terms with this brand new creature in your lives who sucks on the parts previously reserved for you. You might also be having difficulty with sleeping beside a creature who bears more resemblance to a dairy cow than the svelte hen you knocked up in the first place. In your head, birth may have been the watershed after which your old lover would return home: hold onto that concept for a while, you have been conned. There's another character about to enter the multiple personality concoction that unfolds during the birth process—say hello to Big Momma.

Big Momma embodies what it says on the tin. She's big and she's all momma. She is focused on one thing, it's small, it squalls, it shits, and it's not you. Big Momma needs a lot of cushions and a lot of sleep and does not want to know if you grazed your knee in a little tumble playing football with your friends.

Big Momma is an interim character as Mum comes to an acceptance of the reality of the child she now owns. She is fascinating to watch. The woman you knew before is gone, replaced with this big soft pillow who flounces in her bed, coos, strokes baby's face and sighs all the time. She and baby adjust cycles to each other's rhythms while one plugs into the other like a valve onto a bike wheel.

You have it easy right now. Maybe you have to cope with night screaming that doesn't have a direct cause such as hunger, crap or cold, but for the most part you're obsolete as Mum takes care of all immediate needs through her mammoth mammaries and soothing Big Momma persona. You're free to take pictures and swan around, basking in the glow of new parent ecstasy. Savour it.

YOU ARE A SERF
New parent ecstasy is a valuable commodity, one to be cherished for its intensity and its rarity. If things have worked out, you have time off work, the missus is in bed doing her nursing thing, and baby is sleeping and eating and giving you crazy fart smiles. You are free to wander gormlessly through life (one of the few free pleasures left), smiling happily at passing strangers and noticing, possibly for the first time, the abundance of passing buggies. Now, instead of begrudgingly making way for them, you tend to actively engage with the child within, only retreating when it becomes clear that the mother is becoming uncomfortable at the odd man misting up while smiling at her baby. This is a wondrous time, but to fully appreciate and prolong it you must be aware and accepting of your place in the natural order at home. Baby and Big Momma sit at the top of the pile, you scrabble about downstairs awaiting instructions.

'Serf' translates as a slave or a person in bondage or servitude.[2] It's a little bit strong in this situation where you are slavering for attention and vying for approval like a cocker spaniel puppy. In these rose-tinted, sentiment-moistened days you would pay for the privilege of serving mother and child.

Somehow, in the space of a few short weeks, you move from struggling to maintain the physical and emotional harmony of a single large female to gladly whipping around after the same somewhat shrunken form and the brand new additional member of your family. This state of blissed-out servitude does not last forever, unfortunately, but while it lasts it should be used to accustom yourself to as many strange and unappealing tasks as possible, for these will become your staple in future times when the lustre has left them. Where before you had Domino's on speed dial and vaguely knew the whereabouts of a decent dry cleaners, now you cook, clean, wash, dry and shop for little or no acknowledgement. In short, for a brief time, you experience the life of an Irish mammy. You may begin to have sympathetic leanings towards liberation and suffragettes but soon society will grant some freedom back and you will quickly forget the struggle, and for that you will be thankful.

Laundry is the greatest mystery of all family processes. When only the pair of you inhabited the house you could be reasonably assured that two decent clothes washes in the week would maintain your sartorial requirements. With the addition of a third, you would be forgiven for presuming that a single extra spin cycle would keep everyone happy. This ill-informed preconception should be examined more closely by environmentalists as they attempt to ascertain the causes of our continuing drive to global warming despite heightened climatic awareness. For a single-child family needs at least two full washes to be completed each and every day if anyone is to be sure of finding a clean pair of jockeys or unsullied t-shirt on demand.

This equates to a 700 per cent increase in demand on the washer/dryer due to a 50 per cent increase in population. The figures do not stack up, something you will become acutely aware of as the child grows and demands increase. There is a proportionate rise in your electricity costs but you may not notice this due to your anxious attempts to stymie the flow of money haemorrhaging from every other part of your, until now, reasonably managed existence. For this reason, your personally attending to every task is not only a way of contributing but also your only hope to halt the spiral of costs.

Consider too the changing of nappies. For the duration of your lifetime to this point, the only human excrement you have come in contact with (apart from in the cosy confines of the delivery ward) is your own. And while you have adapted that task to incorporate reading materials or visual and auditory aids, and become somewhat inured to your own stench, this is not a procedure you would wish anyone else to be privy to. Without the hormonal rush of new parent bliss it would be a daunting task to face into the multiple changes of leaking fluids your baby demands. Once, in happier, more respectful times, no father would have been seen dead with a diaper in one hand, wipes and rash cream in the other while baby lies contentedly on his shoulder, squeezing out one bomb after another. Now it is a rite of passage, a mark of you as an enlightened male, that you can transfer a stinking, sodden arse into a fresh wrapping while stirring a wholesome stew, ironing organic cotton babygros and polishing parquet floors.

It might seem appropriate to envy our forefathers their freedom from such tasks but in fact these new skills can prove your salvation in future times. At the outset, the first couple of nappies might average a change time in the region of fifteen minutes. Carpets will be stained, walls splattered and linen destroyed, but by the end of year one the attentive and dextrous father can have that time divided by ten if not fifteen, no matter how violent the explosion was. This can buy valuable time down the line.

In much the same way, your skill with the laundry will increase. The time required for launching each wash does not increase with baby's arrival but the hanging of wet clothes takes much skill. Everything is so damn small it requires your fingers to adapt to a different language to unravel and hang the seemingly endless supply of socks, mittens, vests and bibs. Days can pass as you attempt to decipher the maximum drying potential of a single clothes horse. Again, within twelve months, your fingers acquire the speed and deftness of touch of a Parisian pickpocket, once more buying you valuable time.

As with most falls into captivity, how you manage your time becomes of paramount importance. 'If you can't do the time, keep your pecker in your pants,' never rang so true. After the initial flush of enthusiasm fades, your skills will be all that make these tasks bearable. Hone them as you would your ability to manipulate a pool cue or read a competitor's tics at the poker table, they will stand you in good stead when it comes to the point that you attempt to sneak your life back.

SLEEP. *SLEEP?*

Inadequate rest impairs our ability to think, to handle stress, to maintain a healthy immune system and to moderate our emotions. Other typical effects of sleep deprivation include depression, heart disease, hypertension, irritability, slower reaction times, slurred speech and tremors.[3]

Sleep deprivation was used by the Japanese on POWs in World War II, the KGB during the Cold War and allegedly by the British army in Northern Ireland.

Using force to obtain information is specifically prohibited in Article 31 of the Fourth Geneva Convention which states that: 'No physical or moral coercion shall be exercised against protected persons, in particular to obtain information from them or from third parties.'

Why then do babies presume themselves exempt from international law, and what is it they want to know?

Everybody worries about getting enough sleep. A typical water cooler office conversation will include titillating details of tossing and turning all night and not quite being able to nod off. Often the person concerned is a 26-year-old man who leaves his house on a Friday evening to return for a powernap on a Saturday afternoon, only to rise again that night for another 24-hour bout with his peers before finally succumbing to fatigue late Sunday night. On Mondays he keeps it shut because he knows he's struggling for a reason, but he can never quite understand why his sleep patterns are a little disturbed mid-week. By Friday, he's forgotten about his dilemma because the swift half-dozen he hoovered with the lads after five-a-side the night before put him straight to sleep. These fellas don't notice the disdain in the eyes of the slightly older new parents in their vicinity. They don't notice because they cannot comprehend the true pain these fresh parents are suffering.

The American CIA Counterterrorist Centre has attempted to legalise the use of sleep deprivation on suspected terrorist prisoners. They refer to it disparagingly as 'torture lite' and ask, in the fear-soaked post 9/11 culture that pervades that country, why shouldn't they have the wherewithal to extract all possible information from the mind of a potential threat. One can only presume that the CIA is made up of childless men and women who have never seen the sun rise from their kitchen window as an infant screams in their arms.

Being woken every three hours is irritating when it happens for a night, it is wearing when it continues for a week, but it's physically and mentally debilitating when it becomes a way of life. Your new-parent bliss and the unusually prolonged surge of new-parent adrenaline can keep you running like a hamster on a wheel for a couple of weeks but eventually you crash, the wheel comes off and hamster-you hits the side of the cage at speed. And unless you can afford live-in 24-hour childcare there is no escaping this.

Multi-nationals, governments, schools, colleges, hospitals, cars and armed forces are run by parents suffering the same symptoms as those endured by British spies caught disseminating information from Moscow in the sixties. Put into that sort of perspective, it is easy to see how the world functions on an eternal precipice, dependent on the good judgement of those who may simply have had all sense knocked out of them through the act of procreation. Witnessing birth and entering the parenting arena not only shakes up any sense of security about our own existences, but also suggests that the civilised society in which we live is a thinly-veneered coating away from barbarism. For if every exhausted mother or father, recently returned to the workplace, were to make fatigue-induced bad decisions everything could come crashing down. Much as it has done in your heretofore civilised home.

A new baby's cycle involves sleeping, feeding and shitting. Unfortunately they find it impossible, for a year at least, to align their sleeping times with their parents due to their frenetic need to feed and shit. When hungry or filthy they will wake, and they will wake you.

For the first month or so, your new domestic arrangements will buy you some level of sympathy in the workplace, at least among colleagues with kids. Your twentysomething party workmates will simply think you a somewhat sadder twat than you were before. But after a month that temporary line of latitude fades and your workload resumes its usual intensity. This may be down to business necessity, but also certainly includes more than a hint of *schadenfreude.* Every parent goes through the pain, the lack of sleep, the alarm clock shriek of horror that precedes the realisation that you had less sleep the previous night than the duration of a football match and now you have to get up and go to work. Every parent goes through it, and every parent likes to see the next generation suffer as they did, just to stick it in their previously smug faces that when they were standing at the water cooler whining about being tired, having been partying for four of the six previous nights, they had no fucking idea what they were talking about.

For that 26-year old party boy is next year's dad. So, as you stand there cupping your plastic beaker of Ballygowan, with your bloodshot eyes and your puke-stained slacks, wondering if you will expire from exhaustion before the end of the day and listening to this prat harpooning out of himself about how little rest he's had, realise two things. First, that was you one to five years ago, ye prick, and give yourself a slap in the chops. Second, he will be you in two to five years. Bide your time and prepare to make his life a misery. It's what everyone else in the office has been waiting for with you.

You notice it now. The congratulations through gritted teeth, the sly smiles that preceded the fall. The notice pinned up in the canteen requesting a €10 entry fee to predict the date of your collapse at which point refreshments would be made available to fuel the impromptu party expected to kick off around your prostrate form where the winner would receive his prize of a weekend break in a pampering spa. These were all telling clues that had passed over your head because, before becoming a father, you had not been involved in the parent-baiting sessions. You were far too caught up in your own meagre little dilemmas back then to pick up on the tribal sacrifices being made under your own nose.

Work and home become one long blurred mass of badly completed tasks. If you feel hard done by in the office, it is nothing compared to the lack of sympathy at home. You didn't lay this egg and that physical act buys her bragging rights on fatigue for eternity. Eat when you can, sleep when you can, wash clothes, and try to keep your job. In time this too will pass, and as you begin to come to terms with this uncertain new life you have forged for yourself, you can at least be sure that there will be others after you on whose misery you can feed.

LEARNING TO LOVE … YOUR WORKPLACE, THE PUB, THE GYM, OVERNIGHT STAYS IN THE CELLS

For all the fatigue and new impositions on your time and energy, the time immediately following the arrival of the baby coming home is a joyous one. You begin to understand the importance of your position as a father within the family and also within society in general. You may have added responsibility, but you gain respect. At least that is what you expected to happen. The reality is you are everyone's whipping boy, a personal masseur and dresser to your immediate family and a tea-maker and sandwich fixer to the line of visitors that parade up and down to your bedroom where Big Momma is holding court and launching her breasts into the public domain like a latter day Lolo Ferrari. This should only serve to reinforce your desire to escape the house at every opportunity and maintain your sanity elsewhere.

Until this stage of a relationship most couples have a settled way of socialising. They go out together with mutual friends and they go out alone, usually with same sex friends. She thinks your mates are a bunch of drooling, misogynistic apes with mother issues and you think her cronies form a coven with vacuous interests and a collective unconscious desire to break you up. Still, everyone engages in the dance, knows their moves, smiles and gets on with things. A baby in the house affects the whole group dynamic, with the core couple bearing the brunt of the force of the unhinged reaction. But before external parties have any influence, new ground rules for leaving the house have to be negotiated because there is no longer any such thing as 'just popping out for a minute'. For every minute of freedom you aspire to there will be a return demanded.

In the first couple of weeks the chances are she will have little or no desire to socialise. You may be free enough to vacate the premises as long as your responsibilities have been taken care of. You have also to be aware of the condition you will be in on your return. If, for example, you leave after dinner has been served to Momma at 7 p.m. but have to return to assist with a night feed at 11 p.m., you know you have approximately 3.5 hours in the company of adults to aim at, taking travel considerations into account. In the general scheme of things, meeting friends for a gentle evening socialising would be of no great consequence, but when a curfew is issued for the first time since adolescence it has a strange effect on the average new father. Instead of supping through a sociable handful of pints he will vacuum Arthur like black nectar simply because he knows he has to leave at a fixed time.

To the rational mind this is absurd behaviour, but it is the first inclination that new father has lost some sense. He arrives home on time but sodden. He stumbles into the bed narrowly avoiding crushing his firstborn, passes out and snores through the night, of little assistance to anyone. He has kept his part of the deal but he has created bad feeling. Latitude to leave the family home will no longer be given on a whim and instead a competitive instinct to slake as much free time outside is installed. Evermore the 'You had, so I have to have' attitude will pervade and this is of no benefit to anyone.

Before the birth, tripping to Tesco for the weekly shop on a Saturday afternoon would have been about as attractive as stripping a gum for a root canal. It soon becomes a privilege, provided it's done alone. If you've watched saccharine American comedies of the *Friends* variety you may think that babies buy you precedence in the public domain, but you would be wrong. Babies get you smiles and winks and coos and 'ooh isn't she gorgeous, she looks brand new!' but we are an innately selfish race so don't expect to be bumped up a queue anywhere. New babies are a better bet than toddlers on a visit to a supermarket, provided they sleep. If they wake and decide to yowl, you should probably cut and run. However, alone, you can take the time to peruse the aisles you never bothered with before as you seek to kill a couple of hours off baby duty.

Visit the supermarket with good grace. You are fulfilling a vital family requirement and doing it with a smile on your face. Your trips to the gym, to matches on a Saturday, to Jambo's for a midnight pay-per-view heavyweight championship clash, i.e. things you took for granted before, are not vital but can be guaranteed by fulfilling family requirements well in advance. But soon these outings may blur into one. When you haven't slept for a month because of an infant teething you don't care if you're at your best mate's stag and the busty Latvian lapdancer has taken a particular shine to you or in the chemist's buying sanitary towels for your missus—you are somewhere they are not, and it's quiet. And the chemist might let you snooze for a moment in the chairs allocated to people waiting for prescriptions, whereas the lapdancer probably will not.

You may start to enjoy drivetime radio in traffic, get to work early, stay late, smile more in public, help little old ladies, tut at unruly adolescents and generally turn into your father. This is not, as you previously suspected, due to the arrival of a new level of maturity on becoming a dad, but rather down to a realisation that people should be nicer to each other out there, because out there you don't have to tolerate a pneumatic drill in the form of a baby with an attitude revving in your ear for twenty-two hours of every day. No matter how much you love the kid, you have to savour the silence and nurture your freedom.

EAU DE LAIT MATERNELLE AND JEANS STAINED WITH SOMEONE ELSE'S SHIT

There is something invigorating about being comfortable wearing clothes moistened by another human being's bodily fluids. When you can sit in the public domain, look down and notice a babypuke stain above your right nipple, a breastmilk mark on your belly and something suspiciously greeny brown on your knee without a hint of embarrassment, you realise you have passed a particular level of consumer decadence and entered a more spiritual realm.

But there is a fine line to tread here. On the one side you have a man who no longer feels a slave to fashion, who no longer judges himself or others on the newness of their Campers or the cut of their hair, a man who values himself for himself and others for the delight of their presence. On the other you have a parental slob, one step up from street wino, who chooses to use his newly fatigued position to inflict his and various members of his family's body odour on the world at large. The former is obviously a wanker, while the latter is a pig. The truly enlightened new father tiptoes between the two, milking either side for maximum effect depending on the sympathetic leanings of the crowd he finds himself mingling in. For example, sat at a tea-drinking vegetarian lunch surrounded by organic wool-clad tree-huggers the savvy pop will expand on how much he has opened up to the light of the world since adding to its population. The response may be increased proferring of tofu bake but it could result in a legitimate offer of free babysitting. Among hardened drinkers, the cute daddy will lament the loss of his free time, the lack of sleep, his inability to maintain his quality time with 'de lads' and hungrily wolf the compensatory pints placed in front of him. It's about wearing your stains with pride and playing them appropriately.

YOUR FRIENDS REALLY DON'T WANT TO KNOW

However, the subtle dance you perform depending on who surrounds you at any given time is really only applicable to acquaintances, second-tier friends and the in-laws. The truth about your real friends' attitude to your current dilemma is somewhat harsher: they don't give a shit.

If only John Gray had had a good look at how a man's friends and a woman's friends respond to their buddy having a child, we may have been spared decades of this women and men being from different planets twaddle. The ladies are interested, they bring gifts, they stay around, they offer help. And they mean it. The boys have a poke of the child, comment on its misshapen head, unaware of Big Momma's low growl, and ask are you free to go out, anywhere else. As usual there are advances to be made in adversity, and getting hurt by your pals' lack of interest in what you consider to be your masterpiece is a little precious. If you cast your mind back you can probably come up with a few memorable examples of your being less than enthusiastic when handed a new baby: "Fuck that's ugly!" being a common pronouncement by young men unused to the etiquette of baby admiration circles shortly before they're kicked out on their ear. Grow a thicker skin and realise your boys have no idea what to say to you about your child because they have no idea what it does or what the point of it is. In short, they feel the same as you did about every child until you had the pleasure of seeing one of your own make an entrance.

Similarly, curb your need to speak about the child on the rare occasions you slip the noose. Sitting at the bar watching a mid-table Nationwide clash on a Monday evening is not the place to begin to speak to the shaven-headed local youths about the softness of her skin, or how she makes you feel when she smiles at you. There is a time and a place for that but, as a final rule of thumb for this chapter, test the air for the presence of oestrogen rather than testosterone when doing so.

Chapter 5
From Here to Eternity
— Year 1

ADJUSTMENTS AND READJUSTMENTS

If the first month with a new baby in the house is a slap in the face with a wet fish, the following eleven are a continual coming to terms with a fundamentally altered way of life. The initial thunderclap is accompanied by a supporting cast, you have in-laws and supportive friends all concerned that you fare well, but once the shine wears off you're alone in the house with Big Momma and baby wondering how exactly this is going to work.

Obviously you are learning to live on about 50 per cent of the sleep that you enjoyed before, and back then you probably found that inadequate. You are coping with your wallet being emptied onto the counter at Mothercare and the local pharmacy as soon as you're paid each week or month. Your chic and comfortable house has turned into a crèche, with hard plastic toys lurking round every corner to twist an ankle and send you crashing down the stairs. The environment you live in is far more hectic and cluttered than before. Big Momma is focused on baby and the destruction of her breasts and you are running to standstill in creased clothes and the beginnings of grey hair.

These are the big changes. They are showstoppers and there's no deviation around them. The place you live in has changed irrevocably. Your relationship with the person you share that space with is in a state of flux. Thrown into the mix is the cause of this upheaval and a demanding new entity in its own right, new baby.

Everything is currently up in the air while you wait to see how they land. Take some time to see if you can affect how that might happen. Chances are that for that first month you've been so immersed in baby you haven't raised your head to take a look at the world. One morning as you're on your way to work you realise the planet has been invaded by aliens and you're living in a futuristic nightmare that nobody stopped to point out to you.

Stop doing what you're doing, put down the nappy bag and move away from the wipes. Take out your phone and ring someone who has no children. Arrange to go for a meal, a drink, to the cinema. Talk about sport, politics and religion. Give yourself a breather. Bantering with a father in a playground one afternoon, he informed me that he was looking forward to going to the cinema with his wife that weekend. It would be the first time either of them had gone out socialising without their child since her birth thirteen months before.

That's just fucking nuts.

You can choose to disregard the life you had before the birth and invest all your energy in raising baby, or you can start to integrate the two. Explain to Big Momma you have to get out there and encourage her to do the same. Look after the little things that get you back on the road to normality and the big life-altering changes forced on you won't seem so spirit crushing.

GIVING UP YOUR LIFE

Alcoholics in recovery speak about the difficulty of accepting the first two steps of a '12 Step Programme'. These boil down to admitting a powerlessness over the addiction, acknowledging that lives had become unmanageable, and handing all power over to God, or alternatively a spiritual 'higher power' so that sanity might be restored. To the regular bloke living on the western seaboard of Europe, i.e. a half decent functioning alcoholic, these words are laced with fear. What the steps say is you have to give it all up to get it all back. That's a pretty daunting prospect for someone who worships at the altar of Tennents Extra, but it's a little easier for a new dad.

A new dad has his old life ripped away. He has less time, less money, less energy than ever before. The cause of this is paradoxically the joy in this, and isn't about to disappear anytime soon. The mistake the new dad can make is in fighting to get his old life back, because that life is gone baby, real real gone. Walking out the door on a whim with a casual 'I'll be back later,' shouted over your shoulder is no longer an option. Wherever you are going, for whatever your purpose, is irrelevant because now time comes from a communal pot. New dad must adopt a very eastern philosophy, throw off the shackles of his western, premiership-obsessed, lager-swilling past and embrace the concept of the shared pot of time. Especially if he ever hopes to enjoy another pint in front of the footie again.

Give it all up, hand over your power, and be released from your past. In this case, the spiritual higher power to whom you are offering yourself is an amalgamation of the newborn child, Big Momma and the new dad spirit guide, for I can only presume there is one who helps us down the tricky path. Hopefully baby will understand, learn to sleep for more than ten minutes at a time and let you off the leash. Big Momma will realise that if she is ever to regain a sense of fashion that doesn't include a human being hanging off her tit you will both have to re-enter the adult world. And the new dad spirit guide will light the way so you don't run screaming away from your family unit into a vat of cider at the first opportunity, never to return. You will be strong and reliable and reappear, with little begrudgery, at the agreed time. Remember, the pot is communal and you have to share. If you do so willingly, the pot will be generous to you but if you fight, the pot can be merciless and cruel. Time, which until recently seemed a common commodity, becomes precious but if you covet it and hoard it, it will consume you.

This is all becoming very biblical so suffice it to say that to get any time to do your thing you have to be a generous little boy in allowing others to do theirs. That's not so riddled with incense and myrrh. But if you're greedy you will be smote, I tell you, smote from on high!

SNEAKILY TAKING IT BACK

Bertrand Russell pretty much banged it on the head when he said: 'Most political leaders acquire their position by causing large numbers of people to believe that these leaders are actuated by altruistic desires.' Politics is a cynical game, one in which we are led to believe that the well-being of constituents is a motivating factor for our representatives rather than a happy by-product of conjoining factors on the rare occasions well-being improves as a result of their actions. And in many ways there is much to be learned from politicians as you seek to regain some sense of having your own needs met while everything is geared to meeting the requirements of the more important members of your family.

Everybody wants a happy house. As a father you want to be loved and respected by your child and by your spouse, yet you do not want to have to demand that love and respect. Previous generations went out and worked, brought home a bag of money at the end of every week, sat at the dinner table and touched in with the children for maybe a half hour at the end of each day before taking themselves off to gentlemen's or workingmen's clubs where they could mingle with other unreconstructed males out to avoid the clutter and noise of cranky kids being driven into bed. But now that the gender divide has narrowed, you are expected to work longer hours than ever before and still find the time to be a shining beacon of example to your offspring. Much as the Dutch pioneered 'Total Football' in the seventies, you must master 'Total Parenting', which involves you being able to conquer every aspect of parenting Mother does so that you can slip into her routine in a heartbeat should anything interrupt her duties. These duties are of course evenly divided so you too can expect back-up support from her if for any reason you can't complete your shift. But, of course, you will always see out your shift.

The instinctive reaction to this landshift over the past thirty years marks us as men. 'Yeah, nice baby love, well done on that. Now, is me dinner ready?' doesn't cut it any more, belonging as it does to the happy generation of motley ne'er do wells that were our fathers. Soon, not only will we be expected to have the dinner

ready ourselves but, with technological advances, we'll be pushing
the brats out ourselves. But the time to fight has passed, we are
ensconced in the dual parenting culture and can only hope that
through our own diligence and perseverance we find our own way
back to being served dinner on a tray in front of the TV.

Never refuse a task, no matter how hard done by you feel. Do
everything in a cheerful manner, make it look easy. When you're
washing a mess of diarrhoea off you, the baby, your clothes, the cot
and the curtains, whistle. If the child wakes five times in the night
demanding to be reassured and you have a crucial meeting at nine
in the morning, be first out of the bed and don't complain. If the
only way to get baby to sleep is to drive her round for half an hour,
you back her out of the driveway even if you've just finished a ten-
hour shift making deliveries. Make the hard yards, and make them
'altruistically'.

At some stage baby will cry and Mother will hold out her arms,
only to be rejected. Baby will scream, refuse Mother and look for
Dad who arrives and silkenly calms child with a shrug and a 'what
can you do?' look. Mum is now a wounded animal which is not an
ideal situation for the continuing mother-child relationship as it
develops. Dad has made the link that Mum covets and Mum wants
it back. Dad better start getting his ass out of the house a bit more,
better start staying in bed through the night as well. Dad better get
his act together and stop taking the piss and attempting to destroy
the beautiful mother-child bond with his overbearing,
overparenting antics. Go on, get out, go somewhere else and do
your thing.
Result.

COOING, CLUCKING AND OTHER AVOIDABLE NOISES
When my wife was about full-term with our first child, bursting at
the seams literally, one of my best friends had his first. For the first
time in my life I found myself interested in seeing a new baby, for
obvious personal reasons. Up until then, whenever someone
popped a sprog and I was expected to comment, my head would
implode in attempting to figure out something positive to say

about this pink, gurning ball of flesh that, as far as I could see at that time, had no point other than wasting vital drinking money. Now, here was my buddy with this prototype model I could use as a guinea pig for a couple of hours and, of course, I had no idea what to do and panicked.

The missus waddled in, picked up the child, stuck him under her arm and proceeded to gurgle and cluck into his delighted face, all the while letting him suck on the tip of her finger.

Mate turns to me and says, 'They just know, don't they? D'you think it's inbuilt?'

'If it is, it's the first thing she's ever been able to do unaided,' says I, loyal to the last.

The kid is handed to me. I stand, turned to stone and hold him at middle-distance away from my chest, fearful I'll break him. Both my missus, mate's missus and the mate are watching sternly. They tell me to relax, just talk to him.

Talk to him? He's a week old, should I bring up politics or will that be offensive? Nah, googoogoo at him, he loves that. At least smile or you'll scare him.

I try a 'goo', then a 'coo', then a 'ble ble ble'. I feel like a tit. Baby boy starts to cry and I swing him back to Mammy's arms, relieved to be rid but depressed at my future as a pathetic brute of a father.

There are two things at play here. First off, cute as he was, this fella was a stranger. When mine arrived a couple of weeks later she slotted into the crook of my arm like a nook had been built there for her. Second, we boys should never 'goo' or 'coo' and should be slapped for attempting to 'ble ble ble'. It's not right.

We can jig on the spot, talk quietly into the baby's ear, sing and whistle, whatever it takes to make the child happy that is within our range of performance, but we can't be doing with all the clucking. There is our own sense of dignity to think about and there is the child's initial notion of the world to consider. Here he is, unsullied by nurture, a product of evolution with millions of years of man's experience hardwired into his brain—he needs one person to feed him and keep him warm, and another to protect him, preferably wild-haired and bearing a large club with the blood of a recent kill still dripping from its protruding six-inch nails. Instead both parents fawn and coo and baby grows up like a startled deer. Leave the gurgles behind, boys, it doesn't matter how young they are, talk to them in a manly fashion and have some self-respect.

THE ART OF PUSHING A BUGGY AND STAYING MACHO

Probably because so many men were spending their waking hours cooing and gurgling for international recognition, buggy makers thought it was acceptable to start marketing their products at fathers as well as mothers. Once that concept took hold the screw started to be turned and no longer could a self-respecting dad walk a safe distance away from his woman as she hoofed his brood up the road; now he had to actively participate.

Once, as I manhandled our lightweight, aluminium-framed single-carrier, which cost more than many useful second-hand cars, into the boot of a taxi, the cabbie spat as he watched before commenting: 'I've had nine kids. I used dress them in the mornings, get them washed, drive them to school, pick them up, cook the dinner and get them to bed. But I never pushed no bleedin' buggy.'

The old school denounce the buggy utterly. They would rather carry triplets on their decrepit, arthritic shoulders than move them in the purpose-built carriage bought for them. And there's a simple reason for that, and this is never mentioned in the promotional material: you can't look hard pushing a buggy.

You can't be a 'good' buggy driver. It's not like skateboarding where you can hit the park and learn some rad tricks. Even if you think you're a master at negotiating rush-hour people traffic with your monster baby town-car, to everyone else you're a prick with a buggy.

You can't be a suave buggy driver. You have to have baby toys hanging from the edges and you probably have a nappy bag with bottles and beakers visible underneath. Even if your wagon cost two weeks' take home pay and came with the optional sports pack, you're still a man pushing a buggy. Do you really think the 22-year-old wannabe models sipping frappucinos in Café en Seine on Dawson Street are watching you go by and thinking, 'Wow, that's the Kidmaster 2000 with optional footboard. That dad is one hot mofo.' They are, yeah.

If you must buggy push, do it with good grace and no attempt at pretence. Employ a buggy that doesn't demand the width of the footpath and doesn't take ten minutes to fold each time you attempt to board a bus. Choose one with quick release straps to loose the monster and a variety of invisible storage compartments to avoid the carrying of excess baggage. Accept that you look like a gimp and don't try to work it. Be the most polite pedestrian in town and maybe a little swagger will return to your hips. Because, as Shakira says, hips don't lie.

MEETING OTHER PARENTS: KNOW THE SIGNS

We rarely stop to consider our criteria for making friends. In school and college being thrown into the same environment as others pretty much sealed the deal. The process of engaging new people and committing to friendship slows after leaving full-time education and entering the workplace. In work you have a number of possibilities to consider: is potential buddy an equal, a superior or a minion? If he or she is not of equal status, will a burgeoning friendship be beneficial or detrimental to you professionally? If you start to get to know your neighbours, you may do so on the basis of common interests or goals, such as sports or mid-afternoon drinking, which are similar in some respects.

However, no matter what the situation was where you established an initial rapport, there is one simple, hard and fast question you will ask before contemplating allowing this new person enter your circle of friends: is he or she a muppet?

Then we go and have kids and presume that because someone else had children in a similar timeframe to us we should all be great mates with no consideration for the 'muppet' question at all. In this arena, as in so many others, having children makes us utterly irrational. In general, the majority of people out there are to be avoided, and the same applies, even more so, to other parents. In the film *Barfly*, Mickey Rourke responds to Faye Dunaway's assertion that he doesn't like people with a drunken shrug and 'Hey, I like people. I just prefer it when they're not around.' Well, I like other parents. I just prefer it when they're not around.

There is a simple reason for this. Parenting is the most competitive of sports. No matter what you do, there are at least five variations on the way you should do it. These include the top 'em up with sugar route; the sugar-free, fruit is God philosophy; the organic path; the disciplinarian drama; and the *laissez-faire*, hippy freak, let them roam free and feral school of thought. Chances are that wherever you are, whatever you do with the kids, you will approach things somewhat differently to the parents around you. You'll all giggle and guffaw at how your philosophies conflict and how difference really is the spice of life and afterwards go home and bitch about what morons that pair of fast-food munching, Coca-Cola snaffling dickwads were. Because when you make friends for the first time you don't give up all the goods at the outset. You slowly reveal to your new pal what a horrible person you are over time so they don't run screaming to the police. The opposite applies with new parent friends. Within minutes of nodding at each other across the playground you are blithely exchanging stories of burst perineums in childbirth and breastfeeding with mastitis. When this level of detail applies at the start there is nowhere to go but to the brink of despair.

Choose your new parent friends with even more care than you would regular friends. These people may develop into persons of some influence over your children with time, and no matter how well you get on, they will judge you on your ability as a parent, unconsciously seeing themselves as an aspirational point for all other parents. If there's any chance they may grate, kick them into touch early on.

Anybody slightly needy, slightly over-confident, brash, nervous, ugly, extremely good-looking, rich or poor need not apply. The spectrum you should work within is narrow and should be populated by people exactly like you. The reason for this—well, you'll engage in the competitive parenting yourself, it's unavoidable. Better to avoid it by choosing other parents with the same opinions as you so all child-related discussions become redundant. Instead learn to have conversations beyond the same old aren't the kids wonderful or psychotic (you'll choose one stance or the other) variety that we tend to have over and over again. As a rule of thumb, ask yourself if the kids weren't involved would you bother with this pair? If the answer even leans towards a vague maybe not, run for the hills now, before it's too late.

PARENT AND TODDLER GROUPS

Parent and toddler groups must serve a purpose but for the life of me I can't figure it out. They will of course send you in the direction of other friendless, desperate people who have no means of connecting except through their children and if that's the height of your aspiration then crawling around on a mat with strangers and their kids may seem attractive to you. I could never get past the fart theory, i.e. that kids are like farts. You can only just stomach your own. Or Sartre's existentialist take on the prospect: 'Hell is other people's children.' The idea of being locked down with a bunch of rugrats I have no vested interest in and their fawning parents makes me queasy.

Once again the concept of parenting as competition will raise its head. In a P&T group that competition will be intensified as there is simply no other topic of conversation other than how little Jack or Jill is doing with eating random objects off the floor or the consistency of their nappy products.

When the elder child was born we had a fantastic district nurse who used to visit the house regularly. Every time she was in the house she encouraged me to visit the local P&T group on a Tuesday morning in the health centre. Finally I succumbed, thinking it may just be a good way to make new friends of my own and possibly find a chum for the six-month-old terror I was raising.

I arrived to a room full of silent women and babies under the age of one rolling around screaming. The elder didn't want to leave her buggy. I coaxed her out until she eventually found herself on a mat in the middle of the room, studiously ignoring all persons around her and banging a lego man into a lego vehicle he patently was never going to fit into. I smiled and made small talk to all around but there was a slight air of tension as if my presence was unwelcome. Nobody introduced themselves directly, only as Peter's mum, or Hailey's mum, or Latoya's mum (yes, Latoya, it was that kind of group). On saying my name was Adam I was immediately asked what my child's name was. My interrogator then turned to the woman beside her and pointed me out as the elder's dad. It was excruciating.

The pain intensified when the only other dad showed up late. About ten years older than me, he had a superstar greying mullet. The hair on top of his head and to the sides was spiky, but a pony-tail poked from the back of his head that tidied up tresses reaching almost to his waist. He seemed nonplussed to see me there, while the ladies were obviously concerned at his reaction. His son was big, a real crusher, a cute boy kid who liked to eat toys, much to the delight of all his surrogate mothers in the room who cheered him along. I soon realised I had upset other dad's harem status quo and made all the mares frisky, not because they might have preferred me but because they wondered how their stallion could respond to the presence of a young colt. It was a fight I had no interest in and instead made my excuses and left early, feeling as if I were escaping the clutches of a Mike Leigh movie. In fairness to other dad, he seemed an easygoing bloke, just with bad hair. If he was getting off on the undercurrent of Lothario filling that room then more power to him, but it was a scene too chilling for me to tease out.

In the first few months of new parenthood, your friends are a lifeline to an alternative, nostalgic normality. Their concerns may seem trivial to you now that you're living in a torturous, sleep-deprived, vomit-coated state but they are an important outlet. If your circle of friends descends into only those who match you in the breeding stakes, the worldview of the group may be somewhat limited. Obviously, support and advice can be garnered from friends and relatives who have been where you are now, and all this free wisdom should be gratefully accepted, but keep the messy grown-ups in the loop too.

KICKING THE CHILD OUT OF YOUR ROOM

So far in this book much reference has been made to living with a lack of sleep. It is fairly obvious what the cause is and it is also fairly obvious that there's not a whole lot you can do about it. If baby chooses to stay awake all night and scream, you'll be doing likewise. There are a couple of established paths to address this which I'll mention briefly here, but won't comment on as you will most likely be told which approach you're taking by Big Momma.

The 'Contented Baby' school of thought pioneered by Gina Ford encourages a strict regime with a closely followed timetable of feeding and sleeping. If you have an unexpressed desire to control others, extreme right-wing tendencies or are obsessive-compulsive, this could be the parenting path for you. When it works, baby settles into a routine very quickly, knows when it's time to feed and often sleeps through the night from an early age. The downside is you have to behave like an archetypal Victorian despot to achieve this. There is no picking up or cuddling of the child if it is not cuddling time. Cuddling has strict time limits which must be respected.

Contented Baby followers tend to be slaveringly loyal to their guru, Ford, and it has to be said her methods are very successful. Her book sales are impressive too so she must be quite contented herself. Following this path requires a strong ability to stick to a routine from both parents which can make demands at the outset that seem unnecessary but have long-term gains, for example waking your child from a midday nap so they'll sleep better later on when all you want is to have some quiet right now! Right now, please, my brain is leaking from my ears!

But the beauty of Gina's regime is that she recommends having the child sleep in her own room from the outset. This is a classic case of taking a stance at the start that seems to cause more grief than it's worth, but down the line, the freedom of having your bedroom to yourself is priceless. Kids burrow into your room, into your bed, and sink their claws into the mattress to the point that extricating them makes removing the British from Ireland seem like a breezy process.

If on the other hand you don't feel you would have been a particularly effective stormtrooper during the war, you may want to consider other options. Some of the alternatives include regimes (or non-regimes) propounded by the baby whisperer Tracy Hogg and Dr Sears. None of the alternatives ever got the press that Gina Ford did, probably because none of them ever drove parents psychotic with rage at the temerity of someone suggesting that they put their baby back in the cot. Go on, move away from the baby! Raise your hands and leave the room slowly, you punk.

> *They fuck you up, your Mum and Dad,*
> *They may not mean to, but they do,*
> *They fill you with the faults they had,*
> *And add some extra just for you.*
>
> PHILIP LARKIN[4]

You see, once that child is born, even beforehand, we are consumed with guilt. All our parents fucked us up, so we can't do that, can we? The one sure way we have of letting baby know we're not going to screw this up is to show that damn baby how much we love her at every possible opportunity. We're gonna pick her up and drown her in love every time we see her after a prolonged absence of more than four seconds. If that baby so much as smiles in her sleep we're going to pick her up and give her some love to ensure that smile was a good smile, made better by our unstinting love. In case, y'know, she forgets for a moment that she's, like, loved.

Yeah, if you're a peacenik, organic vegetable badge of honour wearing hippy you should probably avoid old Gina Ford and give that baby some love. And prepare to have that baby still crawling into bed beside you when she's sixteen and this time she's crawled home from a party with her friends where she consumed 16 Bacardi Breezers, 37 Marlboro Lights and a handful of magic mushrooms. You want your relationship to be close, but not that close.

You may not have much input as to which tack Big Momma

takes with baby but you have to busy yourself with getting that child out of your bedroom. If it seems a little harsh not to have the cot by your bed for the first few months, fair enough. The kid'll be squalling to be fed and nobody will have to move too far to get her. But when you get down the track a bit, you're going to be looking at Big Momma with more than a little lovin' in mind again and you will want some privacy (more about this vital re-unification in Chapter 7). Also, kids tend to spontaneously spew with alarming regularity, from both ends. It's bad enough cleaning up the mess in their bed, but things reach a new level of nastiness when you're trying to get back to your slumbers where someone else has just defecated, and with the prolonged risk that more is to follow.

Make a concerted effort to plan the removal and be strong about this implementation.

A short summation of the things we like to do in our bedroom makes it exceedingly obvious that this is no place for our children to dwell. Of course, we like to make the good love. Not too well most of the time, but we still call it the 'good love' with a drawn-out Georgia twang to make it sound better to ourselves and anybody who's had the misfortune of doing it with us. We like to scratch, everywhere and with prolonged vigour. Then we like to sniff. We like to chuck one off the wrist with impunity. It doesn't matter how often the 'good loving' is happening, nothing beats the power of your own imagination and a recent smile from a hot neighbour. We like to read with the light on, and those Spiderman comics lose all their edge in bad light. But most of all we like to sleep, and when you've got someone claiming squatters' rights on the left-hand side of your pillow that doesn't happen too well.

In short, it's fairer, more generous and altogether only human to have that baby away from the room where you like to get personal. If you truly want to show baby some love, let her live a safe distance away from you.

MEDICATION AND VACCINATIONS

If parenting is competitive, then how you treat the kids when they're sick is the Olympic Games (but with less drugs) crossed with the Champions League. Before the average male breeds he pays less attention to the chemicals he ingests than he does to style supplements in daily papers. As long as the tablet in his hand does what it promises, it is going in mouth and will be swallowed. End of.

Average male has a baby and he is suddenly expected to be concerned at the make-up of baby meds. Refer to above: if pill or gel or liquid does what it promises, it's going in baby's mouth and nose will be held until the struggling subsides and pill is finally swallowed.

But we're getting ahead of ourselves. It's one thing becoming accustomed to the demands of a new baby, but it's another step towards ecological disaster in the spectrum of climatic change when baby gets sick. No matter what the ailment is they scream and they roar and they holler and they kick and they puke and they shit and all they want is for you to help. The problem is that they can't tell you what's wrong. So, exhausted as you are, you give up any thought of sleep and concentrate on dealing with the small things. If baby is hot you try to reduce temperature, if coughing you try to soothe discomfort, if stomach is upset you try to solidify or liquidify, delete as appropriate. If, when these simple things are addressed, there is no change, you get the fear and bail to your GP or the emergency room. Priorities are on, you may be tired, but baby needs to be looked after even if you're next to certain it's nothing but trapped wind.

So, those are the general rules. Check the simple possibilities out yourself and address them. You're not a doctor but you're probably not a full-time idiot either; if it's a cold a doctor will pocket your cash and tell you to take the screaming beast home, chuck some Calpol down its neck and wait it out. The key thing here is how you approach dealing with the simple things in the first place. Because it doesn't matter what you do as long as you're addressing the problem.

Take one mum, let's call her the Calpol Queen. Child sniffles, it's out with the Calpol. Child coughs and we're onto Benylin For Kids. Temperature rises somewhat and we're talking Baby

Nurofen. Temperature isn't falling, crack out the Paralink suppositories. Throughout, baby is being cleaned down with Wet Ones antibacterial wipes, sanitiser and gel. All good gear, all with one single aim of getting baby better. A little neurotic and over the top maybe, but which mother doesn't become a cloying mess at the first sign of new baby losing the plot?

Next door we have the Pulsatilla Princess (named for the homeopathic remedy Pulsatilla which seems to heal everything from a runny nose to gonorrhea). The child has to be pretty knocked about for the princess to inflict anything on it, preferring instead to use healing foods and herbs and scents. If child begins to deteriorate, further homeopathic remedies will be administered and the leeches will be readied. If the child still fails to improve some chanting, howling, dancing and drumming may be invoked to the spirit of good health in order that baby may once again breathe freely. Whether it's the concoctions, incantations or simple fear, this method has about as high a success rate as the medical version in treating common ailments. The only difference is your homeopathic remedies and garlic pills aren't promoted by multi-billion dollar pharmaceutical companies. No, the alternative approaches are usually backed by slightly crazy-looking women with self-knitted sweaters and a propensity for cats. Which is a PR disaster.

The trick is to agree with whatever approach is prevalent in your household, help in its administration and be ready to move quickly if the child should, for whatever reason, need further assistance. However, if anyone is going to question Big Momma's methods it should be you, because for a stranger to assert that Momma is barking up the wrong tree is a crime punishable by slow death due to prolonged threatened-mother angry stare.

One thing you can't do is assert your approach to another family uninvited. Even if asked your opinion, be wary about being honest, because if your opinion clashes with that of the mother involved you are likely to be seen as a judgemental bollox and flayed before being kicked out the door. Simply agree that everything she has done thus far has been on the money and if you have any further suggestions tiptoe them forward as gently as possible.

The area of health and babies is a living paradox. The area where we need to be most fluid and open to all possibilities is generally the one where we are most entrenched. Calpol Queen scoffs at anything that hasn't been approved by the drug authorities and stamped with a kite mark, while Pulsatilla Princess would rather hand the baby over to wild dogs than introduce a chemical synthetic into its system. As with most things, a meeting somewhere in the middle often works best, but it is important to be aware of the strength of feeling and fear involved on both sides before suggesting there be any loosening of stance. It is a very brave dad indeed who runs the health gauntlet.

This dogged adherence to the way in which we treat our children's physical health is nowhere more apparent than in our attitudes to vaccinations. The number of injections that children are expected to take from the day they are born until they hit their teens has grown rapidly in the last thirty years, with the mantra that 'never before has the number of communicable illnesses been so low' being used to justify each one. Each parent is supposed to hand over their child unquestioningly to be inured against the latest offensive disease with little explanation being offered for the vaccination's necessity.

Some parents choose not to vaccinate, concerned at the lack of available information about the drugs that they are supposed to accept blindly will improve their child's quality of life. These parents are routinely vilified by the pharmaceutical companies and the medical establishment for not only endangering their own children but also putting the rest of the population at risk. Any opposition to the vaccination line is portrayed by the establishment as insanity, and as a result any worthwhile debate on the subject is cut off at the knees. One side adopts a smug, patronising approach while the other is made to look utterly demented.

No matter where you stand on this debate, I think it is safe to say that the huge majority of parents will only do what they believe is good for their own children, and in the same way would never act in such a way as to risk the health of anyone else's child. If we accept that as a truthful premise then it is a simple step to realise that the notion of one side deliberately placing the other in danger is ludicrous.

The pro-vaccination lobby operates on the assumption that these medicines keep children from the risk of some contagious diseases. The anti-vaccination crew strongly believe that the risks involved in taking these medicines outweigh the benefits. Both are attempting to do their best for their children.

The anti-vaccination crowd shout that the multitude of shots being forced on the kids are down to profit-driven pharmaceutical companies who have got into bed with governments and have little to do with the general health of the nation. The proponents shout 'paranoid conspiracy theorists are risking everybody's lives!' They both have a point. It's a freaking minefield of an area, not helped by the fact that the literature produced by both camps is so obviously biased, resulting in a dialogue that never enters a useful middle ground. The huge wealth and power of the pharmaceutical companies suggests that there must be a level of corruption involved; history has proved this an inevitable truth. As such, it can only be wise to weigh up their propaganda carefully. Health service departments are overworked and underfunded and need a one size fits all system to fulfil their obligations without having to attend to a number of individual cases, so the government's motivation must also be questioned. However, the vitriolic stance of the anti lobby does itself a disservice, giving the impression, as it does, that they have no faith in either pharmas or health services despite overwhelming evidence that the quality of our lives has improved immeasurably in the past century mainly because of procedures and gains made and implemented by both.

As a dad it's your responsibility to look after the health of the creature which is doing its best to destroy yours. But often the best that can be done is to voice the alternative perspective in such a way that it is palatable to the policy-maker at home, opening up all avenues of opportunity. My reaction to being told I must, or even should, follow a particular path without any hard evidence to support such a decision is often to reject the suggestion out of hand. It's not a particularly adult approach but it's a suspicion-based model of behaviour drawing on a lifetime of experience. My mind is generally only changed on seeing someone whose opinion I respect and value offering another approach and encouraging change. Is it possible for a slovenly, single-mindedly selfish, traditional auld bollox of a dad to be that moderator? Maybe so.

TWELVE MONTHS AND YOU CAN BREATHE AGAIN

When the elder was born I entered a state of new-parent bewildered euphoria. A couple of weeks later, as I sat cradling my daughter one evening, the wife's uncle and aunt and three kids dropped in. Uncle was looking on as I alternated between singing my daughter's praises and lamenting the end of sleep, and he simply offered the line: 'Get them to one and they don't break so easily any more.'

That stuck, the whole thought of reaching a year and the pressure easing off. And it's true. At the end of the first month, after the steepest learning curve most men will experience, it's near impossible to visualise eleven months later when the suckling, twitching ball of resemblance to you will be a robust toddler. For those initial weeks time stops, you enter a baby vacuum where all that matters is figuring out how this creature works. Then things start to get easier and one morning you wake up and realise you know what you're doing. At that point, the time accelerator kicks back in and reminds you you're pretty damn old and only getting uglier. It's a cruel, miserable, fucked-up world.

Chapter 6
The First Birthday

THIS ONE'S FOR YOU

You got there, buddy, the first year is done! Twelve months ago you were in all likelihood hovering round a delivery ward, stressed and fearful of the unknown. Now you've been hit by everything. You've witnessed your lover burst like an orange, you've taken in a non-paying lodger, you've cut your disposable income in half, given up on sleep and become adept at understanding non-verbal communication. The child that now stands in front of you is nearly 100 per cent recognisable as human. It's time to congratulate yourself, have a party.

Developmentally, you now have a kid who's probably toddling, possibly walking, has teeth, eats solids, communicates freely with you by expressing every emotion to its extreme and sits comfortably at the centre of your world. To measure and note the phenomenal growth in those twelve months can make you gasp— that such a rich and creative little person can now stand there, with their hands out, wanting something, always wanting something, from the tiny creature that burst on the scene such a short time ago.

And it is a short time, even though it feels like a lifetime for you. For others who haven't had the same experience as you, only a year has passed. You, however, have aged dramatically. Those grey hairs that were barely visible before have now announced themselves with a flourish on the areas of your scalp where hair still flourishes. If we are to wonder at developmental advances, some should be reserved for you and the fact that you're still standing despite looking like you've taken a serious beating and morphed into your own father overnight. So take the bull by the horns, clean down the house, invite some people over and make like it's 1999.

Once the decision is taken to have the party, a plan of attack needs to be formulated. You have two broad options. The first is to be stupid and behave as if this is remotely related to the child who is one year old and won't thank you for disturbing his playtime and passing him round random strangers who will leer and poke him. The second is to draw on the well of knowledge you buried a year ago and try to resurrect an ability to have a good time. If you follow route one, there is a host of information available on the web that will guide you in the way of the bouncy castle, hand-drawn invites and petting zoo. You can devote yourself to providing a good time for kids of parents or relatives you vaguely know that are old enough to demand such things at a party. Your child isn't, but will be soon and when that happens you'll have to hire Girls Aloud to keep him happy.

If you go the baby route you can personalise everything from invitations to posters to napkins to thank you cards to balloons, and nobody will give a toss, least of all the birthday boy or girl. One of my favourite tips for invitations comes from the parenting section of the iVillage website:

Use clip art: Find images of (for example) Winnie the Pooh, Teletubbies or Thomas the Tank Engine within a clip art programme and print them out on your invitations.

Think visually: After printing out invitations, cut them into a fun shape—like Pooh, Dipsy or Thomas—around the border.

Make it easy: Many shops stock pre-printed themed birthday invitations.

Review the books: Spice up your invitations by using several quotes from children's books.[5]

Because when you're preparing for a party what you really really want to be doing is trawling through clip art for 'fun' images. But then, after suggesting all the wonderful and fun approaches you can take, the next option is to go and buy pre-printed invites (the sub-text being that only drug-crazed, crack whore parents would let little Johnny down with a shop-bought invitation). If, however, you are a crack whore and must buy pre-printed, do spice up the

invite with some appropriate quotes from your favourite kiddies' books and no, lickle drug fiend, that doesn't mean *Trainspotting* by Irvine Welsh.

How about this. Ring your friends and family, tell them baby is one, you feel as if you've emerged blinking into the sunlight from a long spell in solitary and you want to have some fun. Ask if they would like to join you. You may want to adopt some of the iVillage page's advice when it comes to Thank You cards because, despite the fact that this will not be a kiddies' party, you will be expecting serious gifts from all attendees. It is after all the child's first birthday.

Many people insist on getting a bouncy castle for a first birthday, despite the fact that the manufacturer's recommend-ations clearly state that nobody under the age of three should be allowed on one. You need to be very clear with the man who supplies the castle what your requirements are. About half his trade comes from parties where no kids will go near the castles, which will instead be used as a boozy trampoline by drunken parents attempting to recapture their youth while disguising their bellies as they flap up and down. The bouncy castle man may well have a particular model in his stable made of extra thick plastic that is taken out specifically for your requirements. This model will be grimier than usual, wearing the wounds of previous first birthday parties, and reek of chardonnay and Stella but the chances are it will stand up to your pounding.

So, in terms of recognition that this is a child's birthday, you have organised Thank You cards and a bouncy castle. After that, all you need is to concern yourself with what you and your guests will enjoy. And, of course, who will take care of the child while all this is going on. Come on in, Granny!

WHO TO INVITE

On first inspection this may seem a bland question, but it bears thinking about. Your immediate thoughts will involve your mates, of course, and hers, that's unavoidable. You couldn't have a party without the boys coming round and they'll take the heat off you should the missus's crowd want to engage in any sort of conversation.

After that there's family. The grandparents will want to make an appearance so you should really make sure the whole thing begins between lunchtime and early afternoon as you will want Granny to assume baby-minding duties when things get blurry for you, likely to happen around six. You must tread carefully between obvious manipulation of the older generation's presence for childcare and supply of the best presents, and ensuring that they are treated as the guests of honour. If at any point they feel they are being taken advantage of they will walk. However, Granny and Grandad's love for a grandchild will usually blind them to all but the most heinous acts of desperation. You could quite safely plonk them in the kitchen for an hour making egg sandwiches provided you drop by with baby for a fix every quarter of an hour. Just don't ask them to wash up as well as cater; they will bear one major task but at two they may smell a rat.

If the grandparents are in the loop you can be assured word has gone round about your celebrations. Granny, by now realising that you are never going to lead your country or discover a time travel device, has shifted her focus to your offspring who she natters about relentlessly to any poor soul who happens to stop by. Your siblings will have heard and expect an invite, whether they have kids or not. If childless, they will come and drink, but if they have bred they will bring the brood, no matter what age, and expect that they be entertained. If their kids are a little older, you can expect such siblings to behave in a similar manner to your work colleagues who witnessed you fall apart initially. They have been through the birthday party dilemmas for years now and are looking to soak up some of your discomfort vicariously. Let their kids run riot, point out to your own parents what delinquents that group of grandchildren are, reinforce the wonder of your own brat, and mention a will. Then walk away.

Cousins who you have not suffered in years, since that particularly traumatic caravan holiday in Courtown, will crawl out of the woodwork, dragging their children behind them. This will be Granny's doing as she seeks to pit you against them once again, except now she's not comparing your academic achievements against theirs. Rather she is flaunting your child's teeth against their children's molars. The competitive family never rests.

Over previous weeks you will have been too dumb to keep your gob shut about the upcoming anniversary in the office. As such, female colleagues who you previously would have crawled into a wastepaper bin to avoid will have reminded you that they have kids and they are free that Saturday afternoon. In a fit of gregarious bonhomie you invite them along and in the same spirit tell your boss you expect to see him or her there too. Before you know it, Dave the drunk in the warehouse who breakfasts on Buckfast is on the list and preparing a party piece.

You feel quite chuffed with yourself. You've obviously grown up. You have a wonderful child, you love your missus and now you're mature enough to have a celebration that brings together the three main strands of your life—friends, family and work. That is a great step forward.

The realisation of what you've done will hit in the week before the party. You've brought together the three main strands of your life—friends, family and work—you dumb prick. In a place where alcohol and fuck knows what else will be available. A forum that will include parties you have freely discussed with other present parties, sure in the knowledge that these two parties would never cross paths. How will your mates react on meeting your boss who you have continuously described as being a closet queen or a psychotic maniac with a fondness for panty sniffing? In turn, you have dissed each of your mates to office colleagues, as you stood hungover and nasty by the water cooler on a Monday morning after a particularly degenerate weekend.

Worst of all, your family will be present. Ready and willing to share childhood mishaps and adolescent misdemeanours with your colleagues and friends alike. The same friends and colleagues you have regaled with tales of your dysfunctional upbringing. This is a recipe that should not happen, a bourguignon crossed with a greasy spoon breakfast, with you as the seasoning. Tread carefully.

FOOD AND DRINK

This may be the first time you have had to consider food for a party or, alternatively, up to now when considering catering a party you have outsourced for canapés and sushi. The first birthday party is a lasagne, spag bol, coleslaw and barbecued burgers affair. It's paper plates, plastic forks and Jacob's Creek chardonnay for the more discerning who don't fancy the Polish lager you picked up on special in Tesco. The reasons for this are historically because it's a kids' party attended by adults, but the real reason is because of the diverse socio-cultural group you have dragged together. You have to fall back on the global staples—burgers and cheap Italian. Some will grumble, but everyone loves a burger, especially with coleslaw. It's the law.

You've got to have a cake, preferably made by the maternal Granny and taking a minimum of twenty-four man hours at astronomic cost. Baby will be photographed wobbling gormlessly above the single candle, wondering why these buffalo are chanting at him before being returned to his cot or a granny. Cocktail sausages should keep the other brats at bay.

Booze is the tricky question. Obviously, you buy loads, as much as your budget can stretch to, but it is the administration of the alcohol that is important. You'll have wine, half-decent and half-shit, lager, stout and Smithwick's for that uncle who thinks it's a mark of character to insist on drinking brown ale. You'll have gin, vodka and whiskey, ostensibly for the oldies to sip, but really for the rowdies to get trolleyed on later.

You've had your UN moment and invited everyone you encounter, and some you don't, in the course of a month. Baby is on show and performing with élan, but his afternoon shift will be over soon and Granny is taking him off the premises after tea. The trick is to get every other non-essential ligger out of the house at the same time or soon after so that only the people you and the missus know, and actually like, remain. There are two paths. Adopt a persona of wilful abandonment, become an utterly laissez-faire, debauched rogue and scare them away (a policy that can be upheld by the missus as she ushers the extras out telling them she's worried for you, that the strain has been a bit much lately). Or bore the shit out of them. Chuck them some grub on a Tesco plate, fill their glass once with Blossom Hill and then doze off. Try to cordon the expected late stayers in one area and insist that they do not make eye contact with any of the B-list guests who are being herded away.

Again this is a gentle PR exercise and some compensations must be made. For the sake of your career, which you have jeopardised by having anybody who works with you in the same room as anybody who really knows you, you may have to bite the bullet and have key decision-makers stay longer and be obviously accepted into the inner circle. This is a tricky decision as they will inevitably learn more about you than they have any right to know. You will, however, also pick up some vital tidbits, if the cards are played right, that they will regret spilling. If the boss stays, get him or her tanked. Do not give up on your mission until a moment of excruciating embarrassment has been reached, at which point you know you are Teflon. Any unexpected excretion of bodily fluids is always a winner, as is a teary confession, a sudden collapse into unconsciousness or an inappropriate advance at another partygoer. All the better if that partygoer is an elderly relative. With a condition.

Also, on food, remember to cook the stuff. The last thing you want is a salmonella outbreak and for you to spend the night in casualty with Auntie Margaret and Julia from Accounts.

WHEN GUESTS BRING DRUGS

Oh taboo, taboo, taboo. This is a child's birthday party, how could someone be so insensitive as to drag in illegal substances. The abandonment of naivety! The sickness of it all.

Drugs, as we are told constantly by the press, are everywhere. Except where we are. That is the flabbergasting thing about narcotics—according to all official research, backed up with mountains of anecdotal material, everyone is tooting or banging up, stoned, high, mashed up, tripping out or coming down, apart from the social commentators who write about the topic. Drug use vies with celebrity property purchases/woes as most discussed topic in glossy Sunday supplements. Only the greatest global recession in seventy years has managed to slow the pontificating on what other people are popping, snorting or shooting. Now, in more straitened times, conspicuous consumption no longer makes such attractive copy. But is still serves to distract us from our crumbling economy. Now, more than ever, we need images of demented, drug addled ex-Big Brother housemates or regular folk tripping the light fantastic to cheer us up. The Sundays do their best to satisfy our needs.

Every weekend brings us fresh exclusives on the 'drug epidemic' sweeping the nation. One might deal with a housewife 'who wishes to remain anonymous' detailing how she was presented with a gram of Colombia's finest as a reward from hubby for delivering their first child. Followed closely by the secret confession of a primary school teacher who can only make it through the day with her second class kids on a 3g a day habit. The publisher of this book recently faced legal action for daring to suggest in print that a government minister was in the habit of using cocaine. From this we can garner that everyone is at it, everyone else that is. Drug use may be widespread, but it's still not cool to let your boss know that you've been flying planes stoned or performing laser eye surgery while high.

So, the chances are someone will bring drugs. It's a first birthday party, not a second, a fourth or a seventh. The first is still closely linked to a past life, a time before kids when you had some choices as to how you lived your life. The gathered masses will be split as to those who have children and those who don't, the latter still regarding the chisselers as little more than objects to be negotiated on the way to personal satisfaction. For there is no guest more selfish at a kid's first birthday party than the single, solvent thirty-year-old male. Let's call him Jonny.

Jonny resents that his friends are having babies, it shines a light on his lack of desire to either have a serious relationship (which is fair enough) or procreate (again, fair enough). Jonny resents that fewer and fewer of his original crew are available at the drop of a hat to go out, tear it up and chase hoop. Jonny resents that the average age of his current circle of friends is beginning to be noticeably lower than his own. To compensate, he spends more and more time in the gym, eats healthily Monday to Thursday and has a lower BMI than when he was twenty-two. Thursday to Sunday he canes, and regales you with tales of depravity which you lap up, living through his exploits. Jonny tells you he's envious of you, all that you've got, what he sees as a comfortable, familial happiness. Jonny thinks you're a dick and this is the only birthday party of a child of yours he will ever attend.

At some point, as evening turns into night and the kids and B-listers have been filtered out, Jonny will sidle up to you and comment on your drooping eyelids. 'Matey,' he'll say, 'You're looking a little weary. Tough day, but you did it brilliantly. Congratulations, you must be so proud. I'm jealous. Now, I've got some fucking marvellous barley that'll have you picked right up and we can get this party properly banging. Here ye go.'

And with that a baggy will be slipped into your hand.

You can choose to take it or not—the fact is, it's there. You may take a moral stance and not partake as an acknowledgement that this is about, at some level, your nipper and you want to, in a strangely fabricated part of your brain, feel you stayed pure. An honourable decision, if a little cloudy. You may chuck the bag at Jonny and tell him to get out, which would be a definitive stance if obviously a little out of character considering he felt comfortable enough to offer it to you in the first place. Fuck it, you may be Jonny yourself, going around your guests, offering them boosters like party favours. It doesn't matter, the fact is, it's there.

Kids blur everything. Self-justification isn't an issue for most of us. We can maintain that whatever we do in our own free time is okay providing we live up to our responsibilities, get to work, pay the bills and don't deliberately hurt anybody. We're a morally hazy society anyway, but innately selfish with an eye for a thrill. Then baby comes along and says, 'Oi chief! I can't walk or talk. I can't feed myself or wipe me arse. That's all up to you. You are the boss of me.' And your self-justification goes out the window because you are no longer responsible for yourself alone, and all the edges of the vague moral questions you never asked yourself suddenly come into focus.

Here's a party where you have probably hired an inflatable castle that could serve as a death trap for a one-year-old child. People have handed round trays of hot food over the heads of screaming, running children all day. Most people will have been drinking steadily since arrival and diminishing numbers will have sucked on cigarettes in the social wilderness of the bin area. The child central to all this will have been handed from guest to guest, squealing at the invasion of prying fingers and bleary eyes before finally being packed off with Granny to somewhere he won't bother people as they get down to the business end of the evening. Yet, someone pulls out a bag of coke and we wonder should this be acceptable at a baby's birthday party.

We're a messy lot, us dads. Our relatively straightforward role of disciplinarian and breadwinner has been whipped away and replaced with an unsaid demand that we be all things to all children. That's a wonderful thing, because we can never succeed, we can only go on trying to figure out what path we're on at all. And the true beauty of it is that we get to question all the time what we want for ourselves, under the guise of what we think is right for the kid. So go ahead and blow that baggy up your nose and apply the same moral logic that was presented above. Or choose not to and use the excuse that you have to behave differently now. Either way, baby makes you make decisions, baby makes you think. Baby is demanding, but if baby doesn't make you assess where you stand on certain behaviours then not much else stands a chance of making an impact.

PRESENTS ETC
People bring gifts to birthday parties. There will be massive discrepancy on the time, money and effort gone into the gifts— from the geezer who turns up with a fiver in an old Christmas card to the second cousin who whittled a cuckoo clock out of oak to go on the child's bedroom wall. In order to capitalise fully on this

birthday and keep the path clear for future hauls, be conscious of everything given. Do not belittle the Godfather who either didn't bother or really 'has picked it out but couldn't collect it till later in the week'. Do be suitably grateful to the grandparent who opened a savings account with a large deposit.

The hardest lesson to learn at the first birthday is that none of the presents are for you. Admittedly, you have spent the previous twenty-one months coming to terms with your diminishing stature in the greater scheme of things but this is the first time you have a physical experience of laying on a good time for people and all the goodwill being expended elsewhere in return. It's a useful learning experience to lap it up and move on, without screaming at the world: 'Doesn't anybody understand the expense and effort I went to just to keep you pricks happy and nobody even bothers to slip me a novelty card in return.'

You can only raise the subject of your own greatness by outdoing everyone else in the present stakes. This is why the grandparents have to be watched carefully; with their disposable income they could quite easily trump you here. If they give money, you give more, if they turn up with a bike you better have a car. A puppy? Bring on the pony. Once assured you are number one present giver, the act should be done in the full view of assembled guests, much to the bemusement of baby who would have been as happy to chew on the remains of the Choc Ice stick you finished earlier. Your credit rating is already destroyed after a year of increased spending and diminished earning, you may as well immerse yourself fully in the debt culture by showing everyone what a truly fabulous dad you are.

Keep all boxes and receipts. When the credit card bill arrives you may want to swallow your pride and shoot down to Smyths with a car full of returns.

BIG MOMMA'S DEMISE

So where is the mother in all this? We've had talk of arrangements, bouncy castles, guests, food, drink, drugs and gifts, but not a word of Mum. Maybe because Mum is emerging from her cocoon and suddenly returning to the person you remember from that time before your life revolved around scans or bottle sterilisers.

Big Momma took the horns for a long time but she has now released some control to you. If she breastfed at the outset, she has probably given up the draft at this stage and you now find yourself with the dubious responsibility of managing the hygiene of feeding utensils. You have witnessed her grow, burst, sag and finally resume a shape reminiscent of times past. She has become a whirlwind at which you stand in awe. Where you thought you had become a master of domesticity (no matter how well disguised for personal gain—see Chapter 5) she leaves you in the ha'penny place on anything from ironing to plastering and re-wiring the house. Big Momma was a foodbag that replaced the woman you knew, but the woman who returns is like a hybrid, she has the charm and appeal of the earlier model with all the ability and earthiness generated by the experience of childbirth. After just a year you are still coming to terms with her newfound powers and trying not to let on how intimidated you feel, but you are glad there is at least one superhuman in the house to cope with all the extra stresses that have you reaching for the gin at eleven in the morning.

If the party is a non-event for baby and a source of disrespect for Dad, it may be heralded as a coming out for Mum, a sort of 're-debutante'. She is more frightening than ever, more powerful than ever, less likely to absorb or absolve you of any guff, but thank Christ she's around because you haven't a clue what to do until she tells you. If anything, organise this party and run it to within an inch of your life. Let her put her feet up, she deserves to be left alone.

CATERING FOR THREE GENERATIONS WHILE PARTYING LIKE IT'S YOUR LAST NIGHT ON EARTH

Your first kid's first birthday party isn't much like any other party you will have ever organised and yet it symbolises everything that's happened in the last year. Parties before were about partying, arranging a good time for you and your friends or other grown-up members of your family. The first birthday is about handing over the pleasure to other people and, if you can, making the little one feel good too. You might feel as if you've had to give up an awful lot, but this party can go a long way to making it obvious why that's so important.

When your parents can sit with your friends who in turn may have their kids around, it brings three generations into contact at your request. Your place in this is assured: you're the daddy. Being the daddy is great, being the daddy is what it's all about, being the daddy means you're no longer the bottom rung of the generational ladder—now you're bang in the middle. And that's a sweet place to be. So look at the faces of the people around you, those who came before and those on the way up behind you, and soak it in. All semblance of your life being a rehearsal, of waiting for something to happen, is blown away because it's all happening right now. Rip into it, suck it up, because it may never get better than this. At some point, bounce on that bloody castle with your child in your arms and believe that the good times have come.

Chapter 7

Sex: You Will (Probably) Do It Again

THE COSMO MOMENT

Y ou're a young man. You've had a handful of relationships and a respectable quotient of sexual partners. Finally you've met someone that you really dig. When you look at this girl, you want to stay looking at her, you're not distracted by the blonde strolling by almost wearing a skirt. Yeah, this could be the one.

You met maybe three months ago at a mutual friend's birthday party. There was some kissing and cuddling but the deal was not closed. Instead numbers were exchanged and, for once, you were anxious about ringing her in the following days. After that there were a couple more meetings fuelled mainly by Chablis and Carlsberg but you were fired by lust at first sight. Now that the carnal desire is lifting, you can look at her and know it isn't purely physical.

So when she says she's going to spend Saturday afternoon shopping and asks you if you'd like to come along, you only hesitate briefly before you say yes. Even as you enter new territory, which is a fifth shop in a row, you aren't complaining and are still willing to comment and give an objective viewpoint. She looks amazing in anything, she could stitch up a postal sack and you'd risk sack burn to get in there with her.

Because you're so comfortable with her you feel free to comment when she finally tries on an over-ambitious pair of jeans. The first words that pop into your head are 'Eezeee now, me honey. Cosy up those curves to me but leave those jeans down because Kate Moss you ain't.' It's friendly, it's funny, it's complimentary at the same time as warning her off what's not going to work, and as you open your mouth to say it you are astounded that nothing comes out. Why? Because, my son, you have been programmed. For your own safety.

From the age of ten we have been aware of the presence of *Cosmopolitan* magazine. Initially it was a tease, the probable source of some early and perturbing erections. As you went through your teens and found more effective masturbation material, *Cosmo*, *Elle*, *Glamour* and *She* all took a back seat. But they, and all their guides to her orgasms, and his orgasms, and how to know when he's cheating, and how to give and receive the best oral, and how to be naughty while staying nice, stayed in our peripheral vision. And one piece of behaviour that we were trained over the years to refrain from, by constant conditioning through exposure to the headlines (who in their right mind would read the text?) of these articles, is the suggestion by a male that any item of clothing would dare to assert a greater mass or volume than the exact amount present in any given female. In other words, we all know never to say something makes her look fat.

Even when we try to infer, with the most honourable of intentions, that a certain top is so tight it is causing her armpits to fold over her chest like a second, hairier pair of tits, we can't. When she squeezes her size 12 frame into her sister's size 8 jeans to the point where she looks like a melting 99 ice-cream cone, we know better than to comment. Leave it to her friends to point out what fits and what's embarrassing; she can't withdraw pleasure from them.

Fast forward a few years and there the two of you are, pushing a buggy down a busy street towards Mothercare. You slip an arm round her and she looks up at you with exhausted eyes. She cuddles closer and says, 'Y'know, maybe tonight we could try to … y'know, give it a go. I think I'm ready … if you are. Are you?'

However it's couched, 'Are you ready?', 'Will we?', 'Fancy lashing the arse off me tonight?', it doesn't matter. That isn't the question. She isn't asking do you want to have sex? She's asking do you still find her sexy? With her either engorged or deflated boobs, her punctured beachball belly, her broken veins, her purple stretch marks. This isn't a proposal, this is a test. The slightest hesitation, the briefest flicker of concern, the shortest 'Uuurrrggghh' through gritted teeth will cut her like a sharpened Sabatier carving knife as it bones a chicken. That hurt will be swiftly replaced with anger and your response will be seized upon and used to disembowel you with regularity for the duration of your time together. Which may be shorter than you imagine.

They say when you fall off a horse you should get straight back on again. Well, this horse threw you off however many months back with the warning that your old playground had become a place of work. Now, after that playground has been dug up and hastily rebuilt, she's telling you the swings and slides are once again open for business. The thing is, you've gone off swings and slides, preferring to play footie with your mates, or even by yourself. Would she understand if you just held on to your ball and had a kickabout? Mmm, probably not. You've got to get up on the horse that is this very confused metaphor and give it the ride of its life. You've got to take this threadbare old piebald (to stretch the image further than it was ever intended) and make it a Gold Cup winner at Cheltenham. Conflicted as you have felt with your sexual appetite denied for however long, you didn't imagine that when you got back in the saddle (had to come eventually) you'd be making love to a dinghy washed up on the beach after the mother of all storms. What you have to learn is that while sex will never be the Olympian sport it might have been in the old days, it has to make a reappearance in your lives at some stage. Whether you or she wants to or not, this is a bridge that has to be crossed.

COPING WITH YOUR LOVER AS A MOTHER AND OTHER FREUDIAN REALITIES

You probably know that deep down you're mainly a big baby, but back when you really were a baby, according to Freud anyway, you wanted to make love to the mammy and knock the shit out of the auld fella. It's all a big laugh now, isn't it, but just for a minute take a look at the mother of your child and ask yourself how like your old mum she is. Maybe it's her sense of humour or her outlook on life, but the sad and scary thing is we're attracted to women who represent a lot of the qualities our mother had in our most formative years. However, if it's the way she likes to tickle your neck with her tongue that reminds you of home, you need to find a good therapist quickly.

We can convince ourselves otherwise quite easily, particularly in the early stages of a relationship, but it becomes somewhat more difficult after she gives birth. It's not that suddenly she morphs into your mother, but that all of a sudden she is a mother and the mother you have most experience of is your own. It is a pretty good general rule of thumb, all things considered, not to have any thought of your mother in your head when contemplating sexual activity, particularly after an enforced lay-off. You spent a large part of your life getting her out of your head; introducing her back in at the same time as you are negotiating an altered sexual playing field could be termed psychological conditioning as torture.

It may be that, for the first time in years, your mother is spending a lot of time around your house, helping with the baby, offering advice and support and generally freeing you up while she threatens the bejesus out of the missus (an unavoidable outcome in modern society). Your baby momma will see your biological mother as a threat no matter how well they get along or however genuinely well meaning your old mum is. You can laugh about this and soothe her worries but deep down you're thankful that Granny is turning up and helping out and you may even wish baby momma would listen to her a little more. Simple but essential father rule: never voice this thought, you will be eternally tarred with the mammy's boy brush and drive a wedge between the three of you that will see you aligned with your old mum while baby momma sits seething on the other side.

The most frightening fact is that these thoughts have seeped in. Since the birth you have required guidance and have gratefully accepted advice from the previous generation for possibly the first time in your adult life. It has been priceless having someone around to soothe your concerns when baby's temperature rockets or you are witness to a first nuclear nappy. But the cost of this support is that, for the first time, you have placed your lover in the same arena as your mother. Worlds have collided; like treacle the concept of your lover as a mother may have extended to touch on your unconscious desire for your mother to be your lover.

Eeeoooohh. Put that thought down and walk on by. This hoodoo must be hexed, you need to step up to the plate.

THE RISE OF THE INAPPROPRIATE ERECTION

It's fair to say that after witnessing a birth the last thing on your mind might be bumping uglies with the organs you saw on display in the delivery ward fulfilling their other natural function. But as time passes your own body will start to signal that its natural desires are returning to a functionality nearing normal after recovering from the visual trauma you suffered. Much has been written about how a woman needs to feel confident enough in her own body after birth before attempting to engage in intercourse again, but it is taboo to suggest that we men may be slightly dubious about inserting our most delicate member in an organ that appears to have had a grenade exploded within.

Okay, let's at the outset state that it must be a more daunting task for the woman than the man, but it's no picnic for us either. This is an event that must be approached calmly and gently, where both parties' egos should be shelved and the partaking in the act be placed on a higher plane than any resulting pleasure. One way of gauging whether or not you are ready to step into the arena once again is the arrival of the inappropriate erection.

It's normal to struggle out of bed in the morning with a stiffy. You might even be somewhat proud of yourself for occasionally revisiting your teenage years when one pops up randomly at work. But when you're bending over to conceal the beast within while bathing a baby or making tea for visitors you know it's time to start taking appropriate action. If you can't walk around the house without knocking over lamps on a horizontal plane with your groin it's time to think about harrying Momma into sharing those funbags of hers.

REVISITING THE BATTLEGROUND

If I were a new mum, and I thank some vague divine being regularly that I will never be, I too would be nervous about re-entering the sexual fray. Not only has my delicate and sensitive passageway been ripped apart by the passing of a human cannonball, but I am now expected to resume the frantic groin wrestling that passes for love-making within the Irish male community. But it's not the physical delicacy of this act that would concern me most, it is the level of sensitivity to my needs shown by my partner that would cause me to fret.

In the course of doing a little research for this book I approached a variety of single men and fathers and asked how they felt about sex with a woman who had recently given birth. What was most revealing were the answers given by single men who, although they had not shouldered the burden of encouraging a partner back into a satisfying, post-natal sex life, had usually some experience of sex with a mother. They were willing to gleefully expand on the nature of their encounters and took no little pleasure in explaining the differences between loving a momma and throwing off the covers with a child-free partner. The dads, on the other hand, were reluctant to answer, preferring to keep their counsel as if, now that they have managed to breed, what goes on in the bedroom has achieved a sort of sanctity. As a father myself and having managed to crack the code of paternal silence with a couple of less stoic daddys, I can only come to the conclusion that this silence is less out of respect than shame. We are, it seems, even less considerate and more selfish as lovers (if that's possible), once baby has passed through what were before our own private gates.

Who can blame the mammys for being nervous about resuming action? There are the obvious physical worries as well as the less clear matter of respect. Phrases bandied about during the course of my research included: 'ripped pocket', 'throwing your mickey into a wet welly', and 'if you shout your name down there, expect an echo back'. If the roles had been reversed and someone had spent twelve hours beating our balls with a cricket bat before stretching our member with a torture device until it was misshapen beyond

recognition, would we be in a rush to get back to proving our prowess? And how would we feel about our partner sniggering at our deformity behind her hand? Our egos, fragile as they are, might well be content to find relief in manual dexterity for the rest of our lovemaking days.

The truth is the playing field has been literally altered, as has the rest of her body. There is more of her in places where you might like less, and less where more would help. But you need to go in there like she's Ursula Andress emerging from the sea in *Doctor No* with that bikini ready to be ripped from her, like she's Marilyn holding her skirt down above the air grate in *The Seven Year Itch*, like she's a living combo of Lucy, Drew and Cameron pouting at you from *Charlie's Angels*. This isn't sex for sex sake, this is sex to remind you that you're both more than just parents. This is important sex.

PREPARING YOUR RESPONSE

The night I lost my virginity is burned on the cornea of my mind's eye. After five years of frantic teen masturbation which coincided with numerous fumbles and comic capers involving bra fasteners and the top buttons of Levi's, someone (an actual real girl) had deigned to allow me penetrate her. For about twelve seconds. My longevity in the sack was only countered by my enthusiasm to go again within six minutes. That ratio of staying power to recovery has pretty much remained the same; I can hang in there a while now but need a few nights sleep before considering the event again. Middle age is such a bore.

But enough meandering about my sexual prowess. My point is that when first exposed to what I had so long desired I was a shambolic wreck. Show me the man who wasn't and I will show you a compulsive liar with premature ejaculation problems. Paradoxically, the first time you attempt sex after your child has been born is as close to the very first time as you will get. Not because you're a jittery little puppy, bucking and frisky, but because it feels like somewhere you've never been before. And underneath you is a worried face, worried that she'll be okay and worried that you are too. She's concerned that bits might fall out or fluids may leak, you're wondering if you rub up and down on her like you're waxing a surfboard with your chest, could you touch the sides? Another simple but obvious father tip: do not rub up and down and tell her you're seeking out the parameters. Such an admission will go down like a shit sandwich and it'll be a long time before you have parameters to reach again.

If you've never trod the boards or had aspirations to play the Dane, now is the time to start catching up. When presented with the question, 'How does that feel?' there is no room for pause. You have passed the 'Do Ya Think I'm Sexy?' test, you can't let yourself down here. It may feel like your groin has escaped by itself into an empty gym hall but you need to motivate yourself to writhe like Mick Jagger in heat with a python squeezing up his pant leg. 'Baby, that doesn't feel okay, that feels amazing.' And if you can let out a Barry White style deep throat gurgle, now is the time.

No matter what happens, you must keep up the intensity and ensure that this reaches its natural conclusion. If Momma hears baby coo in the cot beside the bed and moves to check what's happening, you throw her back on the pillows with unrestrained passion. All you may be thinking about is catching some serious kippage before the howling starts again but you need to produce your A-game and kick up some Ron Jeremy style loving.

WHEN YOUR LOVER IS A MOTHER YOU SHOULDN'T THINK OF ANOTHER

Fantasise. Don't hold back on this, if you can't burst the dam on the first one you may be setting a dangerous precedent. Trawling through the internet for advice on the role of fantasy in a 'married' relationship, I got righteously bored. It is incredible how sex therapists, professionals in the area, can make sex seem like the most mechanical and devoid of oomph act biologically possible.

Random quote: 'Studies reveal that people who fantasise frequently appear to have more fun in bed, have sex more often, and women have more orgasms during sex than those who refrain from fantasising about their sex lives.'[6]

No shit? Get a professional in and they'll state the obvious, charge the earth and remove the fun. Which bloke hasn't closed his eyes and thought about another girl? Sometimes we'll go down the celebrity path and dream we're sticking it to Jordan or Lily Allen, but it seems more common for the average geezer to trod the memory route and trawl through the archives for past experiences. Just remember, as you scrunch up your face and get into the whole rutty swing of it, that when she asks you what you're thinking you reply, 'I'm thinking about how great you feel baby' and not 'This chick Lucy Hamilton I scored at a youth club disco in 1989.'

So drag up Lucy or Jordan or the glimpse of thigh you caught getting out of a swish Audi roadster this afternoon around which you concocted a whole scenario while stuck in traffic, and bring them into bed with you and Momma and the babba sitting in the cot staring at you malevolently as you take advantage of what he sees as rightly his. Look Oedipus in the eye and make love to his mum!

EXERCISE

Woman gets fat then has baby. Man has baby then gets fat, and bald and old. How many times have you seen it? You run into Joe at the bar some night and he looks like he's travelled into the future, hung out for a decade and engaged in some traumatic armed conflict before returning sunken and wizened. It's only been a year since you saw him, hands in the air, top off, giving it loads at Electric Picnic and you wonder has he been taking part in some advanced freeze drying tests because he's been short of cash. 'No,' he tells you, 'We had a baby six months ago.'

Let yourself go and you really let yourself go. It's the start of the slide into terminal decline. The kid's keeping you up at night so the only time you have to yourself is in the car on your way to and from work. You think that now you're a dad you should move to the suburbs where there's more room and fewer druglords. As a result your commute gets longer and you start to appreciate Lyric FM. Your life passes as you sit on the M50 with your paunch expanding as you sob to Chopin. You start to wear jumpers and cardigans. You adopt a side parting and spend hours comparing car insurance quotes. Sundays are for gardening and reading the property section of the *Times*. You ride mechanically approximately three times a year.

Get out and get some exercise! Apart from the obvious physical benefits you'll look at yourself in the mirror and think this is the kind of guy who should be making sweet love. It's that or the growth of man boobs and the adoption of string vests and a comb-over, and who in their senses is going to want to get physical with you then?

The other somewhat more sinister result of exercising is that it will encourage her to get the back of her arse up from behind her knees. You can't encourage a fitness regime if you don't lead from the front. It's a ridiculous proposition when put in context— you've quite likely spent your twenties engaging in nothing more energetic than choosing a double in the 2.15 at Kempton, then you pop a sprog, lose half your sleeping hours and 60 per cent of your disposable income, and you have to start working out or running in public to have any chance of a Bonnie and Clyde on a Sunday morning. Pure daft, but essential if you are to fight off the slide into lawnmowing, car washing and lamenting what the kids today are getting into. Because, if the truth be told, you'd like a little of what the kids today are getting into.

Buy a tracksuit. Suck in the gut. Run.

HOPE FOR THE FUTURE

You've listened to the conversation: the missus has a mate around and they're watching TV when Victoria Beckham/Catherine Zeta Jones/Sharon Stone is shown flaunting her size 4 figure at the latest movie awards just six weeks after giving birth. The two women look up from their mugs of tea and bags of crisps long enough to mutter that it's impossible for her to look the way she does after having a baby. 'She's had so much work done. I mean, look at her forehead—you could tell her her legs are on fire and you wouldn't know if she was surprised or in pain. Botox.' The two of them glance at each other, exchange withering looks, shake their heads, sigh and go back to their Kettle Chips.

You sit in your armchair thinking how hot Victoria Beckham/Catherine Zeta Jones/Sharon Stone is looking and compare her with your two lady friends melted into the couch, hair up, sweat pants on, stuffing their faces and thank the Lord you married someone who respects herself enough not to tamper with what nature provided. Botox would be a fine thing. But there is quiet in the room because baby is sleeping so you decide not to risk the atmosphere of bonhomie and say nothing. Besides, if you don't do something about it soon, you'll be able to perch a beer can on the upward slopes of your ever-increasing Ned Kelly. Pot kettle, kettle pot and all that.

At least baby momma has come out of the baby stupor for sufficient time to notice how other baby mommas are looking after their trials and tribulations. The response may be laced with venom but it suggests an instinct for and a desire to look good. At some point down the line the sweats will be put away and consideration may be given to reintroducing the thong. The game may never be quite the same again, but it will be back on.

Chapter 8
Toddling

FIRST THEY GET REAL CUTE

Often, after the first birthday, a sort of metamorphosis takes place. Until now you've been taking care of a baby and a lack of communication has been the problem. You look at this child, you smile at each other, you giggle, you laugh, then without warning the child starts to wail. You've spent a year figuring out what each individual wail is about and now for the first time the child is starting to tell you. Life gets easier.

The first time they stand up, they fall down. They stand up and they fall down over and over again, but there is none of the 'new baby about to break' fear about it. At this stage they have developed wondrous layers of fat, a padding designed to ricochet them from furniture to wall like gurgling pinballs. Injuries do occur, limbs are broken and gashes burst, but for some reason their newly precarious vertical position is less nervewracking to a parent than earlier mystery ailments which often seemed to have no causes and no clues to remedy. You start to take the bumps for granted because you're beginning to relax yourself. Momma chills out too —everyone's having a grand old time.

The cuteness factor is possibly evolution's way of letting them and you get away with how bloody annoying they can be when brought into the open the first time you release them into the public arena. Everywhere you went up until now they were strapped down, first to your chest, then in car seats, buggies and high chairs. Now you go out for lunch and they want to meet other people, more often than not other people who are going about their business with little concern for the wonder and beauty of your offspring. You love the fact that you can once again enter a building for a coffee or a sneaky beer with child in tow, but you have to learn to read the signals as to whether everyone around you is as happy to see you and your newly mobile creature.

Years ago a friend of mine finished college with a mediocre degree in Philosophy and moved to England to do the only job he was qualified for—driving a London bus. At first it was an adventure. He had a big red toy and he got to chauffeur it everywhere with the one proviso that he not kill anybody. For a while he lived the dream, put-putting between Chelsea and Camden and wandering home in the evenings to sip supermarket lager and congratulate himself on fulfilling a childhood ambition. Soon, however, the dream turned sour. The world started to come in on him and interfere with the private relationship he had developed with his bus. No longer was it enough to spark up that big diesel engine in the morning and go rumbling round. He confided in me that his idyll was being spoiled.

'Why?' I asked.

'It's simple,' he replied, 'The general public are a bunch of pricks.'

He would have driven that bus forever and a day if nobody wanted to get on with him, but he had to come to terms with the fact that he was involved in a commercial enterprise and other people needed him to stop, open doors, let them on and take them places. He quit shortly after revealing that he was suffering a recurring nightmare where he stopped his bus, full to capacity, along Camden High Road, reached under his seat to where he had hidden a contraband AK-47, turned and unleashed a hail of bullets until not one passenger was left breathing. It was an image that stayed with me and I did nothing to dissuade him when he handed in his notice. It seemed safer not to.

Not having worked much in direct contact with the general public myself, I couldn't really relate to the extremity of his emotion until I became the guardian of a roaming toddler out in the world. Those pumping, porky legs bring you face to face with the complete human spectrum when you venture beyond your front door. You must cope with the general public, and they can be pricks.

TODDLERS OPEN DOORS

If you operate from the general premise that my bus driver friend was right, then you will work from a position of antagonistic fear. It is probably more appropriate to presume him right, but work on the assumption that he is wrong, if only to avoid bloodbaths. Out in public you need to develop the art of assessing where a squealing mass of self-obsessed flesh that can't sit still and is prone to flashpoints of pure, raw rage is going to be acceptable due to its innate general cuteness and, on the other hand, where it is going to be seen as a direct insult to those around you.

Start with your choice of buggy. A large mountain charger with reinforced, aluminium undercarriage might be wonderful for forging through the Sally Gap on a bracing weekend hike (should that be your bag) but it won't be appreciated as you squeeze up Grafton Street on the last shopping day before Christmas. In that situation a €10 stroller from Penneys is far more appropriate. If you apply the same common sense to other social arenas, everyone can emerge a winner.

On entering an enclosed space you have to imagine the type of person inside and ask yourself are they likely to welcome your presence, maybe ignore it, sometimes embrace it, or possibly offer assistance should things get out of hand. This is always a possibility with a toddler in tow.

Teenage girls may notice a child briefly before returning to deep contemplation about their hair or choice of shoes for their public appearance. You are invisible to teenage boys—you may think yourself reasonably cutting edge and down with the kids but they don't see you. As for the child, a sixteen-year-old boy has as much interest in your kid as he does the affairs of the European Monetary Union.

Twentysomethings generally pity you but will go out of their way to avoid you, unless they are early breeders and can directly relate to your situation. Even then, however, they will be keen to distance themselves from you in an attempt to retain some kudos with their peers.

Thirtysomethings, who I am presuming the majority of Bad Dads are, based on most recent statistical research i.e. a trawl of my mates, will offer some solace. All of them are afflicted by the kid thing. They have either had kids, are trying to have kids, hang out with people who have kids, or are living a wonderfully indulgent and financially secure party lifestyle without any thought of procreation but suffer the occasional pang of guilt and will be willing to tolerate you to assuage any bad feeling. Be on your guard, however, because the thirtysomething can suffer from kid overload, having been completely overwhelmed by the demands of his own, his friends' offspring and his extended family, and as such be desperate to avoid contact with anybody under voting age. If you come across anybody in the midst of 'Little Bastard Overload' syndrome, acknowledge their pain, which you too will undoubtedly sporadically share, and move away.

Fortysomethings are tricky. They may be approaching the end of the kid tunnel and suffering from 'child fatigue', in which case they will have no interest in you and yours, preferring to see you suffer as they did, or they are just as deeply embedded as you (the prototypical thirtysomething Dad), having partied for a little longer before succumbing to nature. In that case, they generally believe they can hack it all by themselves, having that little bit more maturity and added financial wealth. They will always be polite but will make it clear that if any bodily fluids hit their Manolos you will be paying for replacements.

Fiftysomethings will save your life. Their kids are either ignorant, poisonous teenagers (see above) who bear no resemblance to the children they once loved, or have pissed off to college or travel around the world, sunning themselves on Koh Phi Phi courtesy of daddy's credit card. Fiftysomethings will burst a gut to get you settled at a table, to hold your shopping, to quell a rage, to hold the fort while you make an emergency nappy change. They are calm and endearing and you should hunt them out. But beware the one per cent, the ones who deliberately avoided procreation. They are usually discernible by a tendency to wear either ethnic clothing with an African twist, or gear twenty years too young for them. To them you are evil personified, rushing around with your harried face, foisting your gratuitous and arrogant reproduction of yourself on others. It is unlikely you will cross paths with this section of society too often as they tend to spend all their free time (of which they have loads due to being financially independent and retired early) in spa retreats or on helicopters between race meetings. They are the real-life Cruella DeVilles who will curdle your child's blood with one withering look.

Sixtysomething and up. They know you're in the shits but they don't care because they haven't had much sleep due to a need to pee six times during the night. And if you're feeling sorry for yourself for having to change about eight nappies a day, at least you're not faced with the prospect of wearing one yourself. Leave them be.

As with most expeditions, venturing out with your toddler will be most successful if you plot the course of your journey at the outset. Ensure there will be a high percentage of sympathetic faces in most places you choose to visit and let the child's charm buy you a sneak up a queue or a table in a crowded room. Toddlers do open doors to some rooms, you just have to know which ones to push.

Standing your ground on the behaviour of your toddler is another learning curve. Our natural inclination is to physically rip the head off anyone who doesn't bend to marvel at the fruit of our loins, who may at any given moment be occupying himself by emptying the contents of his nose into his mouth. But choosing your battles is a skill to learn, and one which, if honed well, will prove beneficial later on when the combatants might include the school board and/or the constabulary. If someone sneers at you because your buggy skinned their ankle there is no reason to catch them with a right to the jaw because they are less than sensitive to your difficulties. Also, if someone becomes upset after your child has emptied that person's chowder onto their lap while you busied yourself with the sport supplement, again you should apologise and accept blame.

If, however, someone voices their disapproval at the volume of your child's behaviour in a public place where children are welcomed, feel free to give them both barrels. This can serve as a welcome release valve that might alternatively have blown at the child and also provides a reminder that the little people are as entitled to their hollers as much as we are to our peace. Kick the begrudger to touch.

YOUR CHILD AND YOUR JOB

A phrase that has become synonymous with the work/life balance theory is 'wealth creation'. The idea is that at some point in your career you need to generate value in your work in such a way that your work will generate value without the necessity of your presence. As such, you can hope to some day earn your freedom from working to pay the man. This can come through building your own business which will eventually run smoothly enough to continue to create profit without your ongoing input, or become valuable enough to be seen as an asset to be sold. Other alternatives are to create something, a book for example, that will continue to sell long after you have finished working on it, or investing in properties or shares shrewdly that make money in the long term. Then in your twilight years when you no longer have the wherewithal to remember your name never mind what you do, you can rely on an income additional to the pittance the government will mockingly thrust at you in return for a lifetime's taxes.

Unfortunately, the time during which you should be strongest placed to develop your long-term wealth creation often coincides with your children being at their most demanding. This can operate as a driving factor as much as a downfall and it is useful, if you are ambitious in the wealth creation field, to look on your offspring as potential pawns in your game of aspiration.

You're tired all the time because you don't get enough sleep. Your clothes are shoddy and stained from sticky fingers and flying yoghurt. Ideally, you would spend your working hours dozing and trawling the internet for cheap flights away from your family. However, to do this for the whole period that your kids physically absorb you would undermine your potential for career success. Like milk left in the sun, you are about to turn. If you don't make strides in this early-senior part of your career, you will struggle to make inroads later when you will be seen as a pathetic middle-aged, middle-management wage slave. To cope with your family fatigue and still advance in the work world you need to examine your boss's perspective on your kiddie scenario.

WOOING YOUR FEMALE BOSS

Your boss is a woman. You already, despite your right-on reading of feminist texts and attendance at a Germaine Greer talk to impress the girl you were dating in second year of college, feel emasculated. Your boss has achieved a level of seniority despite society placing any number of obstacles in her way so must be regarded as having some sense. Whether she has done it with or without kids is a matter of key importance.

If there are pictures of inanely grinning imps scattered round her desk you can presume not only has she bred, but she is proud of her brood. The pictures though can be red herrings. Where most geezers like to construct their work stations as monuments to minimalism, women will often stick up photos of cute kids they met once at the zoo and random crayon drawings they found on the road. Ensure the brats are hers in advance, or, by commenting on them, you might remind her of her psychotic drive to be a hero at work despite her inability to conceive. Once maternity has been confirmed you need to forge a bond related to the constant struggle it is to give 100 per cent at work while still attending to parental duties. If you can manage to deliver a line like that and maintain sincerity you're halfway to clearing the work decks at any rate.

You must recognise that she has got to where she is despite the added hindrance of childbirth so your commitment to your work must be unwavering. If you can add to this a new-found sensitivity for the plight of all parents based on your recent experiences she might begin to see you as a person with hidden depths rather than the boorish lout she would rather never have employed, who took twenty sick days last year and tends to sleep through Mondays.

You say: 'I want to give my all to little Jonny but also to [insert employer here] and find there aren't enough hours in the day. My wife is the same. She would like to keep working to be an active participant in a more egalitarian society but feels she is letting her child down because she can't also be a full-time mother. It's the old home versus the greater good dilemma.'

You say: 'I respect you all the more because you obviously manage to combine a healthy family life with a successful career.'

You say: 'I think "Family Friday" once a month would be a great idea. Parents can bring in their pre-school kids and they can play together. We can exchange stories and support each other. It would be good for parents and the kids, as well as being a wonderful team building exercise.'

If she doesn't see through you immediately and boot you straight down the stairs you could be in the money. It's hard to be cynical in the face of such sincerity so you must be careful never to let the mask slip. The next time you wake up with a bastard behind the eyes after a quick eight on a Wednesday night and know you haven't even started the report due that day, you can ring in and, without a quiver of shame in the voice, explain that little Jonny has a temperature but you want to monitor him before wasting a visit to the GP.

PLACATING YOUR MALE BOSS

He knows he has you by the balls. His only question is how hard he can twist them without you collapsing.

He's been there. He's relished watching you come in red-eyed for the last year and not budging an inch when you request extensions on deadlines or when you beg that your workload be shared among others on the floor. He understands that you often want to run screaming from the house and most of the time the only place you have to go to is the office, and you can't afford to fuck that up because you have that screaming maw to feed. He's loving it.

You look at him with his red whiskey nose and his Magee suits and his teenage kids and you know that he gets to sleep for as long as he wants because he hasn't had a ride in ten years and nobody wants to speak to him if they don't have to. Yet, you need him.

You do whatever he asks, you make each and every deadline, you become the golden boy. You sympathetically inquire after his pair of misfit sons and nod in all the right places when you hear that Bob has been told his ballooning weight is a thyroid problem and Bill is attending a counsellor to deal with anger issues. You take an allied stance on whatever attitude psycho boss has to his long-suffering wife, probably drinking at home and lamenting her life choices. You wheedle in and when the time is right you strike like a resentful cobra and take the bastard's job only to keep him on in the mailroom to witness you do what he did in half the time for double the profits.

Your boss, male or female, is the eye of your new-parent storm. Use your recently-acquired wily ways to further your career by extending the extra energy required to stay alive at home to the workplace and you will be following in the footsteps of many parentally-crazed luminaries of the past.

YOUR FRIENDS STILL DON'T WANT TO KNOW: RESPECT THAT

Your child's new-found independence, his ability to move around and inform you exactly what product or service he wishes you to provide or perform, may lull you into the mistaken belief that he has finally become interesting to your mates. Up to a point he has; when stuck with him they can now torment him. Without one of their own, they will have no idea of the repercussions of taunting a toddler, the immediate tantrum and the psychological scarring. To them he is a puppy. They can walk into a room and comment on how much he has grown and how much more mobile he is, but once Momma is out of the way all they want to do is play fetch with him. Throw a ball to each corner of the room or garden and have him trundle and retrieve it. This will become all the more amusing if there are obstacles, preferably sharp ones, in his path.

The missus's friends, or your girlfriends if you are metrosexual enough to have any, can pick up bouncing cherub and inquire as to how he is, how his toys are and even go so far as to pick up a book and read it to the child. They like to entertain and enlighten, usually in the misguided belief that he will remember and favour them in the future, but their motives are irrelevant here—they are usually nice to your child.

Your friends, however, want him to entertain them. He is their plaything and they will not rest until he squalls, at which point they will hand him back to you and leave the house before Momma's wrath is directed towards them. The truth is, it's better this way. They are not potential babysitters, they are your alternative to family life, your pressure valve, and it's just as well that they have no interest in or sympathy for your trials at home. They provide an alternative landscape and you need to remember this when you begin to bleat on about how your relationship is developing and how you are finally coming to terms with the overpowering sense of love the father-child bond has brought into your life. That sort of talk will only cause your alternative landscape to pack up and leave.

THEN THEY GET REAL NASTY
It's around 11.30 on a Saturday night and you're sitting comfortably in your favourite boozer having just ordered a last round for the group you're with. It's nice, isn't it?

Earlier in the evening a group of you may have met up and gone for a meal. Someone had recommended a new bistro, the missus had booked a table and a whole gang of people you hadn't seen for a while were free that night and they all managed to turn up. At the meal the conversation was light but stimulating, everyone knew each other and the banter was good. Your food came promptly, the fillet steak melted onto your tongue and the wine flowed. When the bill came the waiting staff had forgotten to add two main courses and a bottle of wine so, as you all divvied up a little less than expected for a change, you felt like you owed it to yourselves to continue on somewhere else. You get to the pub presuming you'll have to stand but suddenly the snug opens up and one of the girls secures it in a heartbeat. You get served at the bar without having to heave through a throng and within minutes everyone at the table is settled and the conflab is off again. It's so smooth you have to check if Carlsberg is sponsoring the night. Good food, good company, happy days.

That's when you should leave. That's when you should hail a Joe, get home, pop a couple of pre-emptive strike Solpadeines and wake up in the morning smiling with nothing but good memories.

But you don't. You insist on going to the club and forking out twenty notes for the pleasure of being mashed into a wall by the sonic boom as you pile your coats and bags in the corner, against your better judgement, because the cloakroom is full. It doesn't cross anyone's mind that if the cloakroom is overloaded, so too is the club and you're all in a potential tinderbox with no way out. You don't care because you're all fighting to bribe the one barman who has assumed presidential status because he decides who gets to drink. When you finally nail him down you presume, rightly, that you won't want to come back so stock up on as many shots as you can down at once, and then carry as many as you can afford back to the corner you last knew your friends to be in. They have done the same except have all got lost and wound up in different corners. There, alone, you wash down your tray of shots, thus emptying your wallet of the deposit for a house you spent four years saving for, and stumble onto the dance floor. You leer at a girl whose boyfriend takes offence. He sticks a bottle in your face, you get thrown out and have to walk to casualty where you wait nine hours to have stitches inserted between your lip and nose by an Indian intern who is out on his feet after twenty-seven hours on the job. As you sit waiting, various texts come in wondering where everyone is. You try to sleep on the hard plastic chairs and only realise your jacket is missing when you look for it to use as a pillow. Your wallet was in it. You ring Visa to be told that €1200 has already been amassed on your card in hotels around the city and, because you rejected their insurance on signing, outraged at the extra €6 a month charge, you are liable for the first €250. You wake up the next day broke and scarred.

Do you see what I did there? I made the night great up to a point, after which it was rubbish. Toddlers are like that. They lure you in with their toothy smiles and their chunky waddles and their great big giggles and you can't get enough of them. The baby is still there but their personalities are bursting out, they want to touch, smell, see, hear and taste everything in their path and they want to share it all with you, to have somebody savour the wondrous explosion of awareness of the world they are experiencing with them. You would crawl over near-molten shards of glass to be in on this because it bursts your heart to witness it. And just when they can't get any nicer, they get mean.

THE TANTRUM

I have it on good authority that the tantrum was invented during the Spanish Inquisition by the Segovian Dominican Tomás de Torquemada as a means to uncover false converts when all other methods of interrogation had failed. A suspected heretic would be left for an hour with a two-year-old who had been told he couldn't have his Lego. After an hour Torquemada would return to find the suspect ready at last to be true to his beliefs. The child could continue for up to thirty-six hours if required but there are no documented cases of their presence being needed for more than an afternoon at any one time.

Without getting too psychological about it, most tantrums are the result of a breakdown in communication between parent and child. An ability to demonstrate their needs to you can be a curse to a toddler because he realises that he can express himself to you, but not necessarily to the extent he would like to. So he stands there with his beaker held out with a charming, aren't I wonderful smile on his face and you know he would like a drink. You fill his beaker and return it to him and wonder why he's going batshit. It's because you gave him apple juice instead of milk. But he's always loved apple juice. He gave it up this morning you moron, he was trying to tell you that now he loves goat's milk. Pay attention, dumbass. Simple nuances like this are the dividing line between a charm offensive and, well, simply offensive. When they blow they blow like Vesuvius. They hit the deck and act all electrocuted and stuff.

THE TANTRUM AND YOU: IT'S NOT YOUR FAULT

Few things get the average Bad Dad particularly guilty, but watching your toddler wail on the floor, scream to hoarseness and speak in tongues can be particularly unsettling. In this way we often mirror the attitude of the child who does of course believe the world revolves around him; he should know better as the world obviously revolves on an axle about his father. We presume it's our fault that this display of primal behaviour has erupted from our previously angelic cherub, and it may have been our fault to begin with. We may have allowed the ketchup to touch the peas, we may have stirred his soup in the wrong direction, we may even have brushed past without stopping to admire him, but none of these events merit the outstanding nuclear response and the prolonged period it is maintained for.

When the tantrum kicks off ensure the child is in a safe position. If you see an accident on the road you are advised to place the injured party on their side so that they won't choke. Don't do this with the child, allow them to find a position with maximum capacity for flailing. As they whip and snarl move padded cushions and clothing around them discreetly, then move as far away as possible without leaving the room. The temptation may be to leave the house altogether but that could have social services down on you. Make a cuppa if it's available and settle down with a paper until the screams subside, as they will when exhaustion kicks in.

If you beat up on yourself over tantrums you are assuming responsibility for them, when all the while the child is attempting to extend the muscles of his will. 'Listen Daddio, I want what I want and you're not paying enough attention so I'm going to kick it right off. Right now and for the foreseeable future.' Also, berating the nipper for losing the plot doesn't help, either the whole thing intensifies or the child is browbeaten into feeling ashamed for his behaviour. That way lies a sullen, shamed child.

Wait it out, check out that night's TV, pick a horse running in a farflung land and be ready to pick the little fella up when he's done. He'll figure it out himself sooner or later; all he wants is to know you're still there even when he's done his worst.

BE THE HERO

As usual, in adversity there can be moments of opportunity. No tantrum needs two parents as witness. Depending on the level of fraying of your and Momma's nerves, have her be the one to suffer the extremities but at the first sound (you will be elsewhere, but within auditory range) of the beast weakening offer to take over. She will have weathered the storm and crave release. You get to slot in at the finish and receive the exhausted, sympathy-seeking hugs and affection as the tantrum winds down. Manipulative? Oh yeah, but who said parenting was fair?

YOUR CHILD: BULLY OR BULLIED?

Continuing on with the theme of justice and equality or lack thereof, it's time to take a look at whether baby is to be more basher than bashed upon. Nobody ever wants their kid to be a bully, but neither do we have any desire for them to be a punching bag. What message should we give out—hit first and ask questions later, or raise the peace sign when under attack? Should you advise caution when little Jonny is set upon by the local trundling two-year-old monster, or should you sneakily demonstrate a teste-twisting technique that will ensure safety and respect in the playgroup?

But before we advance any homicidal tendencies we should probably look at what's going on for baby, and what's changed for him since he started upping and moving, and quite why he may want to start adopting some defensive techniques.

It's a strange old thing, movement. As a parent you realise for the first time that the child can, if he wants, move away from you. That's good of course but a bit hard to stomach. It frees up some space but at the same time the 100 per cent dependence is gone. So what do we do? We immediately palm the little blighter off on the other kids in the vicinity. At any family gathering, birthday party, christening or communion, we'll drop the monkey on the floor, push him in the direction of the other little people, and quickly check out what's on the buffet and if the red is drinkable. We may request some slightly older child to keep an eye; the poor kid aged about four will eye you balefully and agree. So, off your baby goes, into the midst of kiddie society to assume their place on the lowest rung of the pole. Crawling, then shuffling, standing and falling in amongst their peers where some compadres will be amicable and others, as soon as your back is turned, will throw in the digs. Law of the poxy jungle.

Then it happens. Baby gets a smack and comes running, well stumbling, back to you, indicating some chocolate-mouthed gurrier who's decided to whack him around. You act maturely and assure babba it was not deliberate, when you know full well it was, and return to your food, drink and company. Then you see the light of your life return to the fray where he knows he's on his own and do the only thing he knows might protect him. He returns the compliment and lands his first uppercut. 'Go on my son/girl!' you think to yourself as you rush over to admonish him.

As far as I can see, some kids will wind up hitting more than being hit, and vice versa, and there's not a whole lot we can do about it. Getting precious about it won't help. You try to instil some of the laws of society and personal respect, try not to demonstrate the exact opposite in your own behaviour, and help them survive. The ins and outs of the whole thing are a blurred muddle that any dad will struggle to come to terms with. They get walloped and they give wallops, what we have to do is let them find their own way. And not kill other children's parents.

Because whatever approach is taken, the results will be dictated by their personality and can only be guided somewhat by our interventions. Their battlefield is the playground. Ours is the far more subtle, yet just as dangerous, one of the grown-up variety. You may be focused on working your way through a whole tray of lasagne or catching up with old buddies, but hopefully you'll be keeping at least half an eye as to what's going on with the chisselers. Some parents won't. You are the over-concerned, super-vigilant parent of one, they are the worn down, jaded, long-suffering mothers and fathers of three and more offspring. They read the child-rearing manuals that you have scattered around your bed long ago and have forgotten everything in them because they realise that what happens will happen. The knocks will come, the trips to casualty are inevitable, and you have to let the brats at it. They are right. But, unfortunately, this experience comes at the expense of your little trophy's innocence. He is the fresh meat presented as the sacrifice in the arena of kiddie society. You, however much you know this intuitively, still want to kill these parents.

A whole other dynamic starts to emerge at these family gatherings as the child learns to move in the world: parents—bullied or bullying. These experienced parents will look patronisingly at you as you attempt to enforce order in the kiddie realm as they turn a complete blind eye to the carnage that inevitably goes on there. It's this situation, as much as what the kids are up to, that you need to monitor.

You'll inevitably have a father of three boys, who stands with a can of Guinness in his hand, watching admiringly as his brood dismantle with gusto every establishment they enter, public or private. Other children are used as stepping stones and weapons in the personal war against the world that this team of minor commandos are waging. This dad works with his hands, has studied at the university of life, and likes to comment proudly that his boys are wild. Eventually, when some other child's life is in obvious danger he will let a roar, 'Enough!' and his boys will stand to attention, proving that if he bothered his arse getting involved everybody else could relax from the fear that either the house will come down around them or that some child will die.

This dad is a useful ally, much as you will probably want to feed him ground-up glass having spoken to him for any more than ten minutes. For you to counter any of his arguments would probably result in a fistfight, but by at least acknowledging his presence and attempting to make brief conversation he will cajole you into drinking for the duration of your time at this event and also sneer at any suggestion by your missus that you get involved in supervising the kids. The caveman in him can provide some benefit to you.

At the other end of the scale there is bound to be at least one parent who will not leave the kids alone for a minute. They will take it upon themselves to attempt to enforce a utopian vision of society on a gang of pre-schoolers who, though tender in years, will soon see through them for the idealist they are. The adult will rush around bent double, repeating over and over, 'oh, be careful, don't do that, now that's not very nice, take that girl's hand out of your mouth, please put down the hammer.' That sort of thing.

Taking these two as extremes at either end of the public parenting spectrum, your job is to walk the tightrope that exists between the two while ensuring your own child isn't battered to death, doesn't mutilate anybody else, and you don't fly into a rage with the demented individuals some otherwise normal people insist on turning into when children are involved.

ALPHA PARENT OR MR SENSITIVE

Your approach at mixed gatherings will be determined by the parental gown you choose to wear which, in turn, will be dictated by the type of geezer you are. However, previous form does not necessarily assure a similar style of parenting. The most hard-nosed, militaristic lout can morph into a soft as putty daddy, while doe-eyed, metrosexual sweethearts have been known to embrace their inner fascist in running their children's lives. All the parenting guides tell you that consistency in your approach is what is most crucial, but I can tell you that this is nonsense. What is important is doing whatever it takes to make the child like you more than they do their mother.

In this regard, whether you choose the role of Alpha Dad or Sensitive Dad is immaterial as long as you are consistent in one aspect of your approach: you always let Momma play her hand first. Let her fight in the trenches and you be the glamorous flyboy, soaring overhead and receiving garlands and headlines in equal measure. The rewards are obvious. No matter what she does, there will be tears and you will either be the rock they turn to or the sop that soaks them up. Either way, you're not to blame. As the toddler begins to flex his will, parenting can boil down to a headbanging exercise and the realisation that you're cracking foreheads with a two-year-old can sap your own self-esteem. Better let someone else do that and you pick up the pieces.

DISTINGUISHING BETWEEN BEING A PARENT AND A FRIEND, AND MAKING IT WORK FOR YOU!

The above heading would, I presume, fit comfortably into a motivational parenting book. It implies that parenting is a role that can't be equated with previously held positions. It suggests parenting equals responsibility, that this is a realisation you must acknowledge. Yet, the final clause reminds you that parenting can be rewarding.

In case you've opened here or haven't been paying attention for the last 100 odd pages, this isn't much of a parenting guide. And bearing that in mind, I ask you, why can't you be a parent *and* a friend? Some of my best buddies have been aged between two and three. The two defining traits of a toddler, increased mobility and communication skills, make them about the most interesting people you are likely to meet.

They want to get at everything, to go everywhere and they want you to come with them and share their experience. As they see everything with brand new eyes, so too do you. You are their companion as well as their guide, so all the better if you can get down on your hands and knees and witness things from their perspective too. A lot of the time the rage that comes with a tantrum is sparked by the fact that, although you may be looking at the same thing, you're seeing it from way up there and missing what they get at their level. Being consistent is all well and good— always enforcing discipline when certain rules are ignored has demonstrable values. More importantly, so too does showing love and affection, letting them know you're there for them, that they are safe and can rely on you, that you aren't haphazard and won't respond differently to requests or behaviours on varying days. Consistency, while not as important as outdoing Momma, is vital. Inconsistency results in an anxious child, desperately seeking approval and never knowing what will come in its stead.

That's the bread and butter stuff, the hard graft, taking three points on a windswept night in Barnsley after being a goal down kinda stuff. The celebrated and fabled nights, the big wins over Barcelona in Camp Nou, the stuff they remember, comes from getting down and rolling in the muck. They remember it, and so do you. Some people can cook with them, others can work magic with pipe cleaners, card and glue. Some can tell stories and play music, and then some others can do none of these things at all but still fall on the floor and howl like a dog. There's a lot to be said for howling like a dog.

Chapter 9
Toilets

TOILET TRAINING

Your child can walk and talk, feed and dress. But you're still wrestling with shitty nappies, binbags full of faeces and the appalling stink of a mobile cesspit. Most parents will begin to wonder between the second and third birthday if their child is ready for toilet training. This is the wrong question to be asking but it is a useful starting point. Here are a few tips to ascertain whether they are ready to go or not:[7]

Imitates others' bathroom habits (likes to watch you go to the bathroom, wants to wear underwear, and so on).

What kid doesn't? They're the most voyeuristic group in society. If, however, little Jonny is only interested in Mummy's thong you might as well stick *The Wizard of Oz* on replay and get used to a long life of show tunes.

Makes a physical demonstration when she's having a bowel movement (such as grunting, squatting, or telling you).

Again, what child doesn't? From the moment they can grunt, they grunt when they're taking a dump, their faces contort into pictures of intense self-scrutiny and they assume a diffident air of pride at their productions, presenting them to you with the aplomb of a three-star Michelin chef unveiling a new entrée.

Understands the physical signals that mean she has to go and can tell you before it happens.

They know what's going on long before they bother telling you they know. They much prefer to witness your raising awareness, the gradual widening of your nostrils, tightening of the throat and eventual reach for the wipes. At which point they chuckle internally at their mastery of the art.

Dislikes the feeling of being in a dirty nappy.

They may dislike it but they know that squidgy packet is currency. If manipulated it can be spread like butter over arse, legs, clothes and soft furnishings. In the ongoing poo wars with parents, a full nappy is an unexploded nuclear missile. The discomfort is the price of its navigation system.

Has 'dry' periods of at least three or four hours (this shows her bladder muscles are developed enough to hold her urine in and store it).

In order to confuse you, the child may hold her urine for twelve hours, then spend a couple of days peeing incessantly. This is a guerilla war tactic designed to maximise confusion against the more powerful oppressor and perfected by toddlers. Their favourite technique is to demonstrate regularity, then spray freely when they have lulled you into a false sense of security, usually when you make the mistake of letting them air themselves by running around the house nappy-free.

Can walk and sit down.

Really? Marvellous. Insightful. Genius.

The question you should be asking is not 'are they ready to be toilet trained?' It is 'are you ready for them to be toilet trained?' In the narrowest sense, they learn to control themselves to the point that they can let themselves loose (literally) when in appropriate circumstances, but the actuality involves so much more than that. Saying goodbye to hazardous waste being manhandled around your house is the goal, but getting there requires more than the flick of a switch. Are you up for it?

There are all sorts of psychological implications related to when you train the child. Some say if they are taken out of nappies too young they will feel under pressure to perform, which is a burden of responsibility at a young age. As a result, they may, even if they adapt with no particular difficulty at the start, revert to wetting themselves or the bed further down the line. If you leave training too late there is the possibility the child will feel disempowered, start to notice that their friends are out of nappies, wonder why they are not and feel babied. It's the usual concoction of psychological complications that leaves you feeling damned if you do and damned if you don't and, to quote the occasional football manager, at the end of the day we all figure it out. Otherwise there would be nappy anarchy.

You, on the other hand, have to realise that training does not involve a smooth transition from the daily reality of nappy changing to the pristine, Armitage Shanks cleanliness of a sparkling bathroom. There are messy moments along the way.

One of my most vivid memories is of a sleepy stumble from the bed to the bathroom one Saturday morning. I had been woken first by the sound of the elder child doing her usual morning rush up the stairs, then some minutes of quiet when I figured her to be in the bathroom, before she crept into our room and secreted herself comfortably between her parents. Quiet as she was, I had been roused and soon felt the need for the first siphon of the day. Eyes still closed I headed for the kazi. On entering, my right foot landed with a soft, wet squelch. I looked down to see everything below the lower reaches of my calf submerged in a potty full of yellow and brown swamp matter. The drama continued as I failed to halt momentum and slipped, crashing towards the bath as my right foot skidded upward, kicking the offending vessel into the air and spraying its contents over every exposed surface in the room including myself. As I lay there, prone and pebbledashed with poo, I figured two things: 1. Potty training isn't all it's cracked up to be and; 2. There was no way I was telling the missus about this before getting into bed. Quick shower, back in the scratcher, not a word to nobody. It was the weekend after all.

The ins and outs are straightforward enough. You tell the blighters in advance what's going on. You baby-friendly the throne, you plant potties all around the house and, for a couple of weeks, at the first sign of a change of expression on their faces you plant them on something that can take the punishment. There will be disasters along the way, carpets will be spoiled and clothes ruined, but nothing that can't be taken care of with a blast of disinfectant and a good bonfire, and soon it will be as if nappy living never took place. The fun happens when you take them out in public, mid-training.

PUBLIC TOILETS AND DAUGHTERS

You haven't given the nappy bag up yet, in fact it's heavier than ever because you're carrying a variety of clothes changes as well as residual Pampers in case the going gets too tough. So you've braved the weekly shop with toddler in tow and you're standing in the queue for the till with a mountain of consumerism in front of you when the face changes: 'Daddy, I need to go.'

'What, right now? Can you wait five minutes and let me get this sorted?'

'No, Daddy! I need to go now! Daddy, it's coming!' Voice rising, panic looming.

You ditch the trolley to the side, snatch child and run for the Gents. You get there and invariably the smell of ammonia and urine knocks you back out the door before you soldier on. There will be a man standing at a urinal and your daughter will ask if he has a willy like you. Depending on circumstances she may see too much and proceed to ask, 'Why is his willy bigger/smaller than yours?' You don't answer this question, just crash into the cubicle, sit her down, hope you've made it in time and that the geezer outside hasn't taken offence. Then you wait.

She sits there, swinging her legs happily and starts to ask questions. Things along the lines of: 'What's under the footpath? Why do we have blood? Are Santa and God the same person?'

Because as soon as she realised that getting toilet trained was about having to be brought somewhere at an urgent rate before anything was damaged, she didn't celebrate freedom from nappies, she celebrated your renewed captivity. The first thing she realised was you are at her beck and call and she can spend as long as she wants perched and chatting. You will be too afraid to move her on.

This fear passes relatively quickly but it appears the desire to sit yapping on the pot does not. It may not seem the most attractive proposition, but some of the best father/daughter conversations can happen as you are held in thrall as she contemplates life and waits for her bowels to move. Once again, parenting is not the most glamorous of occupations but this phase should provide you with wonderful conversational material for her teenage years.

Boys are faster, in and out with a trail of carnage behind them. Perhaps saving toilet time for later years when they're interested in consuming the Sunday sport supplements. In many ways the gender differences mirror approaches in later life. Going to the toilet will never be a social occasion for men; it's the highlight of many a night for gaggles of ladies throughout the country every weekend.

WILLIES AND BUMS

The fascination with other people's bits and the proud display of one's own parts is a lifelong concern born in the training period. A fascination for a toddler, only surpassed by what these parts produce.

I always believed my own toilet habits would remain firmly private. For a stage during my twenties I had a housemate who liked to continue a conversation either while he was on the pot himself, or he would hover outside the bathroom door and keep talking while I went myself. I always presumed his predilection was the result of a traumatic experience during his potty training but didn't think this was the sort of issue I could raise with him.

However, with children came the realisation that no aspect of my life, my movements, my thoughts or my feelings were any longer my own. When the trials of family life would become over-demanding I would retreat to my usual spot of solitude with a decent book, drop the pants, sit and relax. Inevitably, this would be followed by the sound of small footsteps. The handle would turn, followed by a harrumph of indignation at the door being locked.

'Daddy, let me in.'

'Go away, luvvie, this is Daddy's private time. Please.'

'Daaaddddyyyy. Come onnnnnn. Let me in. I need to go.' The guilt ploy.

'Then use the toilet downstairs.'

'No, Daddy. I need to talk to you.' Quietly, trying to intrigue me.

'Talk to me from there.'

'No, Daddy. I need to see what you're doing when I'm talking to you. Come onnnn!' Becoming frustrated at her inquisitiveness being denied.

'You don't need to see any of what's going on in here. I'll tell you that for nothing.'

'Daddy, are you doing a big, smelly poo?'

No answer.

'Daddy, is it worser than Mummy's vegetarian ones or is it not badder?'

No reply.

'Daddy, if I done a touch of it would it make me die?'

Ah, Jaysus. Up, wipe, buckle, flush, wash, depart. Give up all hope of privacy for foreseeable future.

Suddenly, your mickey becomes simultaneously an object of ridicule and intrigue. You stand in relief, peeing a stream away only to look down and witness a little arm reaching between your legs attempting to grasp the golden arc. You panic and wind up, spraying the walls and yourself.

'Why can't I touch your wee?'

'You just can't.'

'Why can you go standing up and I can't?'

'Just can.'

'Your willy is a silly looking hairy thing. Mummy's bum is nicer and it's not as hairy. You're hairy everywhere, you're like a big dog. Boys' willies are stupid, bums are nicer.'

'Yeah, I know.'

With toilet training, the toilet becomes the centre of your life. If you're not running to it, you're talking about it. If you're not talking about it, you're thinking about it. Your last bastion of peace has been invaded. You may not have to face nappies any more, but nor do you have anywhere to hide. It's a tough trade.

TOILET TALK IS NOT DINNER PARTY CONVERSATION

If you've learned anything, you've learned that no matter how intrigued you are by your own child, you leave your admiration and concerns and delight at their traits behind you when you enter adult society. Nothing bores the soul more than being stuck at a table, or in a corner of a boozer, with an over-enthusiastic mother or father gushing about baby's gummy smile while checking with the babysitter every six minutes. Although some slip through the net, most people know this. They acknowledge that when people ask how the baby is at the start of a night they are really offering a window of a couple of minutes to get the goo out. Then they expect you to shut up and consider something mutually engaging. It's a polite thing and it does us all good.

The whole toilet training scenario catches us unawares with regard to the child discussion in public rules. My theory is that because, for the first time, the child is a verbal communicator in a particular developmental phase, we as parents forget that this is still a child-related issue that you and maybe only someone else going through the exact same thing will appreciate. So we find ourselves blathering on about how we came to the decision to get little Jonny out of nappies, we include some hilarious anecdotes about his fun-filled nappies in a variety of public places, and move on to the latest round of stories concerning little Jonny and his adventures in Pottyland. Before we realise it, we have been talking for an hour. About shit, basically.

That is not to say that some people will not appreciate the topic. These people will lap it up, encourage you on, hoot with laughter through every brown-stained tale. These people will go home by themselves and attempt to light their own farts while watching MTV and smoking joints. If they are the people you find yourself hanging with on the rare occasions that you get to go out, you'll know something has gone wrong. You also have to wonder why, when you spend all week wishing you had more time to be with people who you can rely on not to leak bodily fluids randomly, you then insist on speaking only about the scenario you wanted to escape in the first place. Open up a can of religious or political intrigue instead. You'll make more friends.

TOILET TALK IS THE FUNNIEST THING IN THE WORLD

Having said all that, farting will never cease to amuse. It's like a personal pleasure, something that continuously cracks up the offender while allegedly disgusting the witnesses. At least until they have a chance to turn criminal themselves, at which point they will heave and strain to vein-popping point to outdo the previous offender. It's a game that brings us back to our childhoods. Among the boys, we take pride in our own stench, as well as great pleasure in inflicting discomfort, if not outright pain, on our peers.

In this way, toilet training provides a pointer to the societal nuances that parenting implies. We have children, we are therefore responsible by necessity. We have children, we are crazy about them, but we realise that not everybody else is and so adhere to their needs as much as our own. We have children, but still like to behave like children as often as possible ourselves. We have children who are as fascinated with farting and shitting as we are, but we have to tread a fine line between outright encouragement of bodily functions as sport and highlighting the private nature of such exertions in polite society. Toilet training provides us with an opportunity to exercise our inner adult, while at the same time providing a huge bank of dirtbag stories to be told behind closed doors. In gourmet terms, it is fusion time, a marriage of the filthy adolescent and the serious adult. It brings out the man you think you want to be while letting loose the boy you hope will never go away.

WHY 'PULL MY FINGER' IS IMPORTANT

It was the American baseball legend Babe Ruth who made 'Pull My Finger' famous. The obese and alcoholic Ruth could fart at will, making friends with children across the nation as he encouraged them to pull his finger as he parped in response. As his sporting prowess faded, so too did his ability to control his sphincter. According to the bio-pic *Babe*, it seems he was almost as disappointed not to be able to blow the hair back from a six-year-old's forehead as he was at his inability to continue belting the ball out of the park. He loved making the kids laugh. The press portrayed him as a buffoon.

There are many things you need to teach your kids—a sense of self-worth, truthfulness, responsibility, loyalty, commitment, hard work and not to jump out of open windows on the upper floors of houses. You do not need to teach them the joys of farting, or belching for that matter. It just so happens that you will enliven their lives, and yours, if you do. Out in the world they need to know what is polite and acceptable. They have to be comfortable when they make their first forays into other people's houses that they won't be ridiculed for their behaviour. But they have to have fun.

And what's more fun than belching the alphabet at the dinner table? Or letting out long, reckless farts in the living room while Momma attempts to watch a movie? You and the brats then go into convulsions as Momma admonishes you for inappropriate behaviour while burying her head in cushions to avoid any noxious fumes.

It's like dancing in the kitchen the way you never allowed yourself dance in clubs. It's like sticking chips in your nose at dinner and continuing to eat nonchalantly. It's allowing the child to steer your car down a country lane. It's taking a chance on a seriously steep hill with a rickety sleigh when it snows. Everything can backfire, everything has consequences. In a way, although every guide will tell you consistency is the key to good parenting, you're teaching double standards from the outset. They have to know they don't let rip in church and not to pour gravy on their heads in a restaurant, but for the sake of your sanity and theirs you all have to be able to let rip literally. Everybody's got to pull the finger.

Chapter 10

The Possibility of Another

IT MAY SEEM LIKE A GOOD IDEA, BUT SLEEP ON IT

As I opened with a description of two slightly contrasting approaches to getting pregnant, it might be worthwhile to revisit those scenarios and examine the altered approaches to achieving the same goal for a second time.

SCENARIO 1—JIM

'The alarm. Jesus, it's the alarm! The *alarm* is waking me up. That's Ian Dempsey, Ian Dempsey talking on the radio is waking me up. Brilliant!' Your thoughts filter through your head in a joyous riot of technicolour. Nobody or nothing had disturbed you during the night, no screams or demands, no nappy to be changed or bottle to be given. No child had climbed into the bed with you and insisted on returning to sleep with head on one parent and feet on the other.

You creep out of bed and tiptoe to the child's room. He's still, thumb in gob, bunny under the arm, lost in his own world. You sneak back to your pit and have a thought that hasn't crossed your mind in a long time. You nudge her, ignoring the sleepy odour rising from her lumpen form. She stirs and removes a strip of hair from her mouth.

'Whaddaya want? Go away.' Charming.

'Nah, listen,' you say, 'We've cracked it.'

'Huh?'

'He slept through the night. He's still inside, out cold.'

She sits up, looks around. 'You're serious. Bloody hell!' Quick glance at the clock. 'I just had eight hours sleep in a row. Fantastic.' She stretches, smiles and immediately crashes back into the pillows.

'No, c'mere missus. Don't go back to sleep. I have an idea.' You sneak an arm round her and give her a tweak.

She rolls over and props herself up on an elbow. 'Do you remember what happened the last time you fancied a cosy morning fumble? We're still coming to terms with it two years later.'

'Come on my love, you know you want it. This is a celebration, he slept all night in his own bed! We should be swinging from the rafters. Come on, come on, come on, just giz a kiss, just a quick one, das right, ooh come on.'

'Be careful this time, ye bollox.'

'Course I will.'

Six minutes later.

'You bollox! Ye feckin eejit, could ye not have held off. Jesus!'

'Ah, don't worry. Sure what's the worst that could happen? And even if it does, sure what matter? He needs a brother or a sister.'

'You bollox! Go down and make me a cup of tea, ye cheeky little fucker!'

'I will yeah, just giz a couple of minutes, just a doze before he wakes up. Cheers.'

And off you go.

———

It can be that easy. One morning you wake up and the strain is gone, you no longer feel pulled taut and it dawns on you that you've got it sussed. In a sort of strange version of Stockholm Syndrome you begin to yearn for your erstwhile captor and immediately presume that having a baby back would be a good idea. Your own child, while still hugely demanding, no longer needs hawk eyes on him at every moment of the day. He can occupy himself for periods of time and you have begun to read again. You have a working knowledge of current affairs. You can hold a conversation that goes beyond feeding habits, sleeping and toilet training. You're a newer, wiser man.

You can go out in the evenings, either solo or in a pair, and know that he'll sleep while you're gone. The boundaries of your world extend once more beyond your four walls and the job. The first reaction shouldn't be to close them off again but, Christ knows why, that's usually what we do. Wiser my arse, you're as dumb as ever.

Having said that, the inclination to reproduce shortly after getting some perspective and freedom back suggests a hard-wired altruistic side to us that most Bad Dads like to keep buried. We justify thinking about 'going again' (I love that phrase, it conjures up images of hopping, shaken, off a rollercoaster and screaming, 'Brilliant! I'm going again.') because we realise that the nipper deserves a sibling. He shouldn't have to grow up listening to your constant bleating and not have someone to beat up himself. We dress it up as the child's need, not our own to have a small baby in our arms again. Whether it's the child's need or yours doesn't matter, the new baby doesn't need to be born. Someone has to make it happen and that person is you so, needs or no needs, it's your decision.

SCENARIO 2—FRANK

'I've been thinking,' she says. 'We can't fuck around for much longer, we'll have to get another one on the boil.'

'What are you talking about?' you say, emerging from the spare room. Your daughter has decided that when she comes into the bed at night she wants your pillow. You thought the first few times that she wanted to cuddle close to you, but no, she wants you out. Her mother's daughter. You fought it for a while but realised soon enough that the only way you were going to get any kippage was to admit defeat gracefully and hit the sparesie whenever she landed in. The obvious alternative was to kick her back into her own bed and you tried that a few times. She screamed in a particularly accusatory manner until her mother came and picked her up, shooting you daggers for whatever unknown heinous crime you had committed. This always happened at four in the morning and you always had a breakfast meeting coming up.

Now, you're sleeping like a kitten in your own domain every night. You've taken to letting the missus go up ahead of you in the evenings and, when you're sure she's comatose, you have occasionally picked the child out of her bed and plonked her gently into yours. You can then slip straight between the crisp covers in the spare room; nobody's the wiser. You view it as the application of Just In Time theory learned in Marketing back in the Smurfit School brought into the domestic realm. You can't tell anybody about its application, but still you feel rather proud.

'We've got to go again. She's growing up, she needs a companion. Only-children and eldest kids who don't have a sibling before they reach five are notoriously precocious but this is countered by a propensity towards depression and/or anxiety in teenage years. Sheila has been telling me.'

Sheila is her latest life guide. A psychotherapist/life coach with a particular interest in spirituality and crystals. Her word is gospel, for this month at least.

'I dunno, love, I'm just getting used to the arrangement we have. And our little baby seems happy enough.' Said little baby is hovering among her mother's skirts, looking at you curiously. She doesn't remember going into your bed last night. She knows you're up to something.

'It's not about you. Not everything is about what you need.'
Oh Christ.

'I suggest you stop being so selfish and consider your daughter's needs for a change. When I get home from work tonight, we're making a baby. Now come on Poppet, let's get some breakfast into you before Daddy takes you to crèche. Hurry up, will you, I have a full day and you're standing around dragging your feet.'

You hit the shower and start the process of coming to terms with being told you're going to have another child. It's simple really, you tell yourself that was what you wanted all along and by the time you're washed and dressed you figure it was your idea in the first place. Besides, you think, at least you're getting lucky tonight. First time in a while.

SHORT-TERM TRAUMA V. LONG-TERM DIVIDEND

For some dads there's a conscious thought process behind having additional children after the first. It usually works along the lines of providing companionship for the existing monster or aiming at getting one representative from each sex. What always seems strange is the lack of thought given to such a decision considering the huge weight of philosophical discussion there was about the first.

Having a second child seems obligatory. You've popped the cherry, your world has been turned upside down, and everything that has happened has been down to the arrival of a small little parcel of human. It is the most divisive experience in most people's lives. The majority of people balance the rush of love with the wash of despair as their money and independence slips through their fingers like sand, the kind you buy for a sandbox in Nimblefingers. This kind of knowledge comes with the role, it is an example of how certain knowledge, such as where to buy sand, replaces other information, such as where is the hottest club this weekend, as kids infiltrate your life. Yet, even though we despair as much as we rejoice in this change, we barely give a second thought to the addition of another.

So, what price the only child? For a start they have a stigma. Other parents get nervy around them because they know their kids will probably bash them and the only child's folks will take the hump at this. That stigma, in a chicken and egg type scenario, then becomes self-perpetuating by the very way that kids and parents tread around the single nipper. The child is bound to behave somewhat preciously as she doesn't have anyone to knock the edges off, she'll have difficulty sharing because everything is hers, she'll have an initial superiority complex having had her brilliance insisted on forever, followed by later experiences of anxiety at not living up to that implied, singular genius. She won't have playmates at home, she'll spend all her time hanging out with you and Mum and picking up all your bad habits, and she'll expect the moon on a stick when she stamps a foot. An only child is a pain in the ass.

But it's not her fault that she doesn't have siblings or that she's so bloody irritating. Nor is it your fault. So when you're deciding with so little thought to grow your flock, give some thought to the alternative and consider keeping it in your pants, or at least keeping it covered when it comes out. If you're going to be methodical about the whole operation, calculate the time and money another child will cost and ask yourself 'is it worth it, just so the one brat I have won't be hated by everyone who meets them?' Break it down into time and numbers and it gives the decision some sort of solid, fiscal shape. Then you'll go and ignore the sensible option and do what we all do, breed on!

It may look like an altruistic decision to have number two and more, but really it's another example of our long-term planning. Get a couple or a trio together, and while they'll only cost you the earth in the first couple of years, at least they'll dig each other out later on. They can look after one another, play together, fight together, rely on each other. And for those periods when they're relying on each other, they're not relying on you. You can go drink pina coladas and watch daytime TV.

It's an evolutionary developed process to have more than one, for the simple reason that they'll look after each other down the line. There is also a far higher chance that, way down the line hopefully, at least one of them will feel inclined to look after you when the spittle is running freely down your chin and the only thing you look forward to is night-time medication and a bedbath on Tuesdays and Thursdays. The more brats you have, the more you have to invest, the more chance one of them might pay you back. It's the long game, and it's more unconscious than we think.

Besides, this is Ireland, procreation is what we do. Keeping the family down to one kid without a valid medical excuse implies to everybody you have a hidden wardrobe at home that you like to raid when the place is quiet, experiencing the light frisson of chiffon on your skin and the dramatic effect of a spot of rouge to your cheek. Just the one child marks you as potentially Protestant, it's not the Irish thing. Get the kids in, and while you're at it, get the round in.

ATTEMPTING IMPREGNATION—IT'S NOT LIKE THE FIRST TIME

I love *Cosmo*. I love its advice, especially when it runs features on 'Keeping Your Marriage Fresh' or 'How To Please Your Man After Ten Years Together' or even 'Putting The "Arr" Back In Your Marriage'. The models they use are always about twenty-three and straight off the beach in Cannes with implausibly toned abs and firm buttocks. They are about as far removed from sex in the marital bed as space travel.

Who here was a Lothario to begin with? Who didn't learn their lovemaking techniques from the readers' letters in cheap British skinmags smuggled home from the UK long before the internet opened pornography up to the world? Who then only ever got to hone their techniques when souped up on pint bottles of Bulmers, with hairy, desperate girls who would occasionally stoop low enough to reach into the gutter to pick you out and take you home? Too much? I'm basing this on friends' experiences rather than my own, which of course centred on romantic dinner dates, champagne and roses. I know most Bad Dads won't relate to that so I am approaching the theme from a generic angle; forgive me.

We were, most of us anyway, rubbish in the sack to begin with. So, when things get cosy and familiar and finally wall-to-wall full of baby gear it's hardly likely that we're going to up the ante and get all Casanova on the female form lucky enough to wake beside us. We're a scratchy lot, not too given to changing the sheets or showering regularly. We like to sleep when possible and smile when awake. Chandeliers are for black and white movies, not for hanging from. Wives and girlfriends are for making breakfast and snuggling into when they say it's okay. And I might push the boat out here and say that breakfast comes a little higher up the totem pole. Sex is great, but we have no inclination for it to last any longer than ten minutes, at a push. Sex is even better if it's a slow, languorous, post-brunch ride on a Saturday with *Football Focus* in the background, both of you getting what you want while lazily figuring out in your heads what you might do for the rest of your day off. The boy Lineker urging you on. But if couch sex in front of the footie is one of the first casualties of parenthood, where then for the love-starved mum and dad? After a period of time together, sex assumes the role of a comfort blanket in a relationship. We turn to it, hold it, rub it and love it for succour. When baby comes along all comfort blankets belong to him. We have to work for our comfort, and we're a bunch of lazy bastards.

We may be lazy but we're adaptable. Once the theme park is open for business again we want to get back on the rides and we do so under cover of darkness. We grab the couple of spare moments in the morning before work, or the sleepy fumble last thing at night, and we do it without noise, a silent passion with a half ear out for footsteps on the landing. We employ no extra accoutrements, only our imaginations, and what goes on there is our own business. You can pack a bag for St Vincent de Paul and into it throw furry handcuffs, novelty whips, garter belts, your Rampant Rabbit and your Big Boy, burn the redundant library of paper porn and recycle the Gimp mask. You are on a strict clock now, and the alarm wears nappies. Remember those furtive creaks from your parents' room many years ago, as you lay awake wondering how you could convince your old man to buy you an Atari? Remember how you devised a strategy and decided now was as good a time as any to visit him to explain how you would pay him back over twelve years out of your lawnmowing money? Remember how he roared at you to 'Get out!' and you wound up with a chess board that Christmas? Well, you're the daddy now and you must strive not to scar your own child's psyche. Keep it quiet and keep it quick. Should be no problem to you.

But getting her pregnant brings another variable into the equation. Just as you began to get accustomed to this underground regime, and had conquered your phobia about shagging with your socks on, you both decide to give it some gusto and do it for the reason God intended. The initial reaction is wary—last time out of the traps she developed a riding timetable to coincide with her ovulation patterns and you wound up feeling like a performing dog in a seriously sick Dutch movie. Rest easy, this time round it's different.

God obviously has a sense of humour because the chances are Momma will wind up in the club if you throw an Allied Irish off the wrist in the same house as her and don't clean up carefully. You can take your charts and your wild yam and Vitex, and you can forget about her tilting her crotch towards the moon post-coitus to encourage conjoinment. All you need do is slip into your usual three thrusts and a grunt and it's over style. If you haven't bagged the produce it'll work its magic, it knows the way.

And we wonder why subsequent kids feel let down? When they're old enough to complain, they whine that there's nowhere near as many photos of them as of the eldest, that they get stuck with hand-me-down clothes, that they've been sent working down the mines since they were six while the first one got to study for exams, that they have to make the beds, cook the dinners, neuter the puppy and sort the laundry. It had to happen—they were conceived as an afterthought on a wet Sunday afternoon because there was nothing but *Songs of Praise* on the telly. They're lucky to be kept around at all, the money they cost.

THE NEED FOR RENEWED RESOLUTION IN THE FACE OF INSURMOUNTABLE ODDS

Although the decision to have more children is often taken with far less thought than the first, there is no reason not to prepare for how the new member will affect your lifestyle. This arrival, and any subsequent ones, will be less of a drama than first time round but any old territory you have managed to claw back in the time between births will be under threat. Looking to the future, you need to plan how to retain your liberty.

You have a life that right now directly involves three people. Much like the exponential growth of laundry when a baby arrives, the demands on your time will increase in greater proportion than just the addition of a quarter to your responsibilities. You'll have all the new baby duties to consider but be aware also of increased demands from the elder (whose position will be under threat) and pressure from the mother who will expect at least some time to bask in the equivalent amount of reflected glory she experienced first time round. This universal admiration never materialises (see Chapter 12, The Arrival of the Interloper) and so mother may suffer a sense of neglect which she will of course blame wholly on you. Your back must be broad enough to assume all extra workload and individual psychological crises while also coping with your own potential mental and physical meltdowns.

The baby will come and will not know that he's there for everyone else's benefit. He will expect and need the same level of care and attention as his predecessor got and probably won't be aware that he is expected to slip into the schedule of the house as has been mapped out thus far. He won't give a shit about how things are done, he'll make his own rules.

You can't know what his rules will be. Whether he'll be a sleeper or a wailer, whether he and the elder will co-habit in harmony or face off like factions in the Middle East. All you can do is wait and see, then give everything you've got, and when some sense of normality resumes remember that you will want your life back once more. If the passage is smooth and you attend to the constants in the equation, you have a good chance of coming up for air within a reasonable time. You can't concern yourself with the variables such as health and temperament; they are the curve balls he'll throw at you to see how much you've learned.

Your return to the waters of baby rearing may be made nonchalantly, but once back in there you still have to swim. And you have to do it with another little face in your face. Prepare for the sleepless nights, re-acquaint yourself intimately with the washer/dryer and the steriliser and look forward to hours finding space on radiators for tiny socks. This time round you have no excuse to be surprised, you walked into this with your eyes open. You have no right to look for sympathy from the masses and the masses won't pay you no mind. If you fuck up, it's your own fault.

Chapter 11

Terrible Twos and Torturous Threes

THE RETURN OF SLEEP—A FALSE SENSE OF SECURITY

Being two gets a lot of bad press. You're expected to fly off the handle without cause, you presume attention from everyone in the room is focused on you, you scream when you like something, you roar when you don't. You have the temperament of an international supermodel, pretty much. Just far sweeter.

Other adults, not directly in your line of fire, coo, 'Ah the Terrible Twos' on witnessing the primeval outbursts. They cluck and mutter sympathetically, then whisper to their friends on the side, 'It's the parents I blame. No discipline, you know. Gave him everything he wanted far too young.' Then, behind the hand, 'Druuugs!'

It's expected, this rage. It's what kids do when they're two, and parents have to bear the strain. The FA Cup final has just kicked off and your team are two up within twenty minutes. There is a chance they may win their first silverware in seventy years and the pain of your teenage support may be alleviated. Your Heineken is going down easy.

In strolls two-year-old daughter. 'What you watch, Daddy?' This is a perfect moment, the child you worship present when your side finally delivers. Your joy can transcend relationship boundaries and crystallise in a memory that will carry her through the ages. She will know happiness for sharing this moment with you. You start to explain, imbuing every pass with a sense of occasion, every shimmy with the hipsway of genius.

She looks at you and nods. 'I want to watch Dora, Daddy.'

'Not right now, luvvie, this is the final. Daddy's team is winning.' Don't you know. She doesn't.

Meltdown. Complete disintegration of her fragile being because she wants *Dora the Explorer* and her selfish bastard of a father is watching football. There is no middle ground to be gained, you can't plead extraneous circumstances, she wants Dora and you are in her way. You bite it down and deal with the situation, it's okay —you can wait another seventy years.

Forget all that crap about 'When Sharks Attack' and 'When Animals Attack' the Discovery channel peddles at you—what you need to be concerned about is when two-year-olds attack. Usually when you're primed with a cold one, horizontal on the couch on a Saturday afternoon. You deal with that, it's part of the regime and all the parenting books warned you about it as well as every parent you've crossed swords with in the last two years. The problem is the twos don't go away on the third birthday, they become more nuanced. Now you have a child with a decent command of English and the ability to play for periods of time alone. She goes to bed at a reasonable time most nights and stays there until morning. In many ways she is a rational human being and you feel that you are sharing the house with another person. She's still close to the twos though, she can turn it on in a moment, reducing you to a gibbering, demented fool, gasping for understanding, anything to make the unannounced rage stop before other people start to point and whisper. She has learned how to use her power, quietly, carefully and only when it will have its most devastating effect.

WITNESSING THE RAGE

The first tantrum is a momentous occasion, coming, as it usually does, after a period of doe-eyed cuteness, a period when you can't drag your eyes from them for fear you'll miss the latest in a series of sunshine-trouncing smiles. The anger comes suddenly, in direct proportion to the new boundaries being opened up to the child. For a while everything was available, everything they wanted anyway—to walk, talk and be involved. Then more is required, more food, toys, TV, more everything and the word 'no' comes back into play. Except this time the denial is understood and taken personally and the response is new. The response is angry rather than just a physical feeling. And they kinda like the way this crazy anger makes them feel and they think, wow, this could be handy. So, it goes on, and on.

The first one causes a sharp intake of breath, like the first sighting, in the flesh, of a beast that until now you had taken as part of folklore. It takes a long time for them to be normalised, for you to accept that it is not in fact possession, but rather an acting out due to denial. At first you're concerned they'll hurt themselves, followed at some distance by a worry about other people and your property. It's a distinctly alien phenomenon to witness closely.

The fuse is irrelevant. It can be the wrong TV programme, the wrong dinner, the wrong step taken on a walk, the clouds aligned in a dissatisfactory manner. There will be an expression of disgust which you may respond to. Your response will be disregarded and there will be a dawning that whatever you do or say has no impact here—the storm is coming. Now the cause is already forgotten because the tantrum has commenced. There is flailing and roaring and gnashing and no response to the usual bribes that can often buy you at least a couple of minutes. In the privacy of your own home the tantrum can be closely monitored for the physical reaction it is, in the public arena of the supermarket you feel like you have been caught berating the child with a birch rod. Unfortunately, how you feel, or who you are, is unimportant. The rage has to pass like a tsunami, and if that bothers people around you, well, fuck 'em. It bothers you a lot more.

The disempowerment is crippling. You can try sympathy, empathy or your own angry response. None will have much bearing until the thing plays itself out, and in the time that takes you can feel the touch of despair at having no ability to alter the way your child is feeling. Through babyhood you can narrow down your kid's distress to hunger, thirst, pain or discomfort, even without the benefit of language. The tantrum is their first warning shot to you that you are far from all-powerful. They lose track of what's ailing them, so very little you can do will alter the outcome. It's a procedure, a roaring process, an indicator of your lack of control. A great sign of what is to come. A humbling reality check for the tenuous hold we have on sanity in most aspects of our outwardly orderly lives. Bless the tantrum, it's a pity we can't have them ourselves.

THEY LEARNED IT FROM YOU

The most frightening outcome of the tantrum is the realisation that most of their techniques are learned from you. Okay, we don't tilt our heads back at a 90 degree angle and scream, but that's about the only part of the rage explosion we don't actively engage in. It would probably be healthier for ourselves and those around us if we were to vent in that way rather than bubbling and venting intermittently like a pressure cooker.

Nothing places a relationship under more strain than the arrival of a child. More often than not the basis of the coupling is exposed for the sand it is. Two people wind up looking at each other over a cot at four in the morning and wonder what they saw in the grizzled visage that meets them. And worse still, it's that person who got you where you are. All their fault, nothing to do with you.

The battle of fatigue is a silent offensive. If you have to state continually how tired you are, you're not really that tired. You must be able to engender your exhaustion into the core of your being, others must become aware of your physical decrepitude simply by experiencing you entering a room. Your sigh must carry a weight you cannot hope to carry. The winner is the parent who can carry this off without actively expressing that they are struggling in any way.

Because this is a passive war there is no outlet for your aggression. You cannot be seen to be hurt. Like any bloke we must crash on in our world-weary way, hoping that someone will understand the cry for help that is our baby-stained clothing and come rescue us. Of course they never will, our fall is far too entertaining for the gathered masses. Of course, if any sympathy is to be offered it will be to the mother who will trump you every time with the act of birth. You are and always will be a sideshow in this child's development and its effects. Your pathetic attempts to garner support from your filthy T-shirts and hangdog expressions are doomed as they have been for generations before you.

Instead, you seethe. You are tired and balance that chip with one on the other shoulder that states you are unappreciated. You work and you father and nobody cares. Boohoo. You seethe and you stew and rather than express your dissatisfaction it seeps out in poisonous little snippets of bile when you can't halt the mask from slipping for a moment. Everyone knows how you feel and nobody cares because that is the order of things and they have either experienced it before you or know they are somewhere in line behind you, still enjoying themselves with sleep-filled concerns and long, uninterrupted conversations about their problems. Everyone knows how you feel and understands and may not like the way it makes you behave but they hope it will pass.

Everyone except the kid. Who gets that you're pissed a lot of the time but can't let on that you are. Who gets that you respond inappropriately and irrationally to occasional situations and has some sense that your inconsistent behaviour is somehow linked to her. Who sees you have all the hallmarks of a tantrum without actually having one, and thinks, 'Maybe I'll have a go at that.' And without your ability to put a lid on it and internalise all that wonderful angst, the tantrum is born.

ZEN AND THE ART OF NON-BABY BATTERING

Accepting that you are responsible in some way for the tantrum is reflective of every aspect of parenting—you are responsible when things go wrong most of the time. But accepting responsibility doesn't mean it's your fault, rather it acknowledges that you're involved. Whatever your kid does, at least until she goes out the door and gets polluted by the whole bundle of contradictory variables she'll encounter in school, is in some way a reflection of how you and her mother behave—singularly and as a couple. Hands up everyone who thinks they have it sussed when it comes to 'being' and even more so when it comes to 'being in a relationship'. Not so clever now, are we?

Frightening as it is, when that child is out in the world she is giving away clues about how things are with 'er indoors more readily than any appalling mess you could make. Her happiness, her joy, her anxiety, her woes are all tied up in how things are going at home. So when she kicks off, you need to be ready to admit you have a certain part to play in her rage against the machine, and also use it as an opportunity to see if you can make things better.

I can't stand advice. When someone offers it to me I automatically presume they haven't listened to a word I have said, instead preferring to sit back and wait for a moment in the conversation when they can interject their telling wisdom. In *The Devil's Advocate* Al Pacino, playing the devil, says, 'The worst vice is advice.' He's right. Take this whole book as a railing on the nature of fatherhood; take no advice from it or take everything in it as gospel (though if you do, probably best to let social services know). It's up to you and good luck to you. Nassim Nicholas Taleb, author of *The Black Swan*, suggests that when people pester you with advice you remind them of the fate of the monk Ivan the Terrible, put to death for uninvited (and moralising) advice.[8]

Offering advice is to presume that you know better, to presume that the object of your wisdom cannot confront their conundrum at least as adequately as you can. It is a supreme arrogance, and this is no more perfectly demonstrated than with the anklebiters. Trying to explain to a two- or three-year-old that they shouldn't be feeling the way they do, or that their response to the way they are feeling should be more controlled or more measured, is nonsensical. They have yet to fathom the varying intensities of emotion they regularly experience, nor do they quite understand why they have been led to understand some things are good and others bad, some right and others wrong. You wouldn't advise a friend who had just lost his wife in a car crash that there is a particular way he should feel and an appropriate way of behaving. To a kid of three, losing that last snack bar can have all the emotional weight of losing their mother, if only for a second. Their reaction is accordingly huge and you have to bear the brunt of it.

The kid kicks off and you see it through. This may involve holding them so they don't hurt themselves or just staying with them until the rough seas are calm. Sip a cuppa, check out the news on Sky. What are you going to say to them? What are they going to hear? Send them to their room, or the naughty step? Yeah, okay, Mary Poppins, do it if you must, but stay around them. Once the whole thing gets rolling they don't care about what they've done or what's been done to them, they just want to kick the madness out. Your job isn't to stop that or encourage it. You're the dad, your job is to be there. Adopt a Zen smile and suck it down. That crazy yoke is your offspring—aren't you proud.

Grannies are great for this, which can only imply that once upon a time you were a champion tantrum thrower yourself. As you skirt around a fuming kid, intent on destroying Granma's bone china because they couldn't have that third bowl of jelly, Granny pipes up, 'Sure, let him at it. They're only plates my ancestors saved from the bailiffs after being evicted by the absentee landlord during the Famine years.' Grannies can be a little over-indulgent on the little ones, particularly if they are the first grandchildren, but in general they are a good yardstick for when you need to cool it and stop getting wound up. Grannies remind you about the fun you're supposed to be getting from the monster, about how much you love them, and about how much worse you were at that age. Grannies know how tired you are and will always have a bowl of soup ready. Grannies rock.

EXACTING LANGUAGE

There is a tendency, because a child doesn't have a huge vocabulary, to speak in a vague manner to kids in the belief that if you were to extend your own verbal skills they wouldn't be able to follow. It makes sense, you can't expect them to respond to you with subjunctive clauses and abstract thought, but the problems arise when you dumb down and presume they won't understand the message you're trying to convey. Whatever language you use, they will make sense of it. What they won't understand is your muttered, vague warbling, followed by your heightened frustration when they either refuse to do what you've asked or completely ignore you because you are patently a cretin.

The way you speak to the kid is important. You're going to have near-overwhelming urges to speak like they do, to repeat their mispronunciations and get your friends to listen to both the child speaking and you providing a replay in Dolby. That is one reason for not doing this, as you come across as a gobshite. As a rule of thumb, remember that things you find cute are cute, but mainly just to you. In fact, your repeating the allegedly endearing behaviour is a little nauseating for anyone in the vicinity not related by blood.

But this isn't the main reason to avoid the cutesy speak. Your kid doesn't get that you think it's brilliant that he says 'mogo' instead of car, or 'gaga' instead of granny, or 'dumbass' instead of dad; he thinks you're taking the piss out of him. He thinks you're a lumbering fool who guffaws moronically every time he opens his mouth. Okay, appreciate his verbal deviances, but speak to him like a normal human being. The upshot of adopting the role of Dr Dolittle for under threes is you will have a kid who quickly gets fed up listening to his old man speak. He'll shut down and go talk to his mother who he knows listens to what he has to say and occasionally gives him a rational answer, and maybe even an ice-cream.

It's easy to be clear to a kid, it's just like being clear to an adult. In the end, they'll thank you for it and so will every other grown-up who has to bear witness to your hilarious sins against speech. Issue instructions gently, using the language that you have honed throughout the majority of your life. With any luck your child will respond in a number of ways. For a start their language skills will improve and they will begin to communicate back with you more effectively, resulting in a more harmonious familial environment. Second, you won't sound like such a gimp and may consider getting your self-respect back. And, third, and this is a long shot, but it may be the start of a mutually respectful relationship based on honest and open communication.

Between a father and son? Who am I kidding?

TRAVELS OUTDOORS WITHOUT HOMICIDE

In Chapter 5 I examined the challenge of entering public life with a buggy and a baby. There are particular difficulties intrinsic to that situation such as the paraphernalia required, the need to have access to food at all times and the possibility that bodily excretions can be sudden and very public. They are all very real and important considerations, but oftentimes they can be overcome in the public arena by the innate cuteness of the baby, and a general feeling of goodwill towards the parent of a new baby.

Somewhere around the standing upright and walking phase, that sense of sympathy evaporates. When you enter public places with your pugilistic mob you are immediately resented. The fact that they insist on shouting instead of speaking, that they resort to screams at the first slight, perceived or real, and that they are mobile, rushing from point to point with no care for others or what they might be involved in, marks them out as Saturday afternoon destroyers. The fact that you are their guide marks you out as responsible for the devastation usually caused.

Personally, I don't like going anywhere with them at this age. Well, that's somewhat untrue and unclear—I get a great thrill out of being with the kids, I just don't like the places I feel obliged to bring them. I'm not hugely active, I don't want to go running up and down hills marvelling at nature in my spare time, I don't fish or sail or build things with my hands. If there were a nuclear strike tomorrow, I wouldn't survive in the aftermath where the practical will overcome. I like to go to quiet places, to read and speak to other people who like these quiet places too. Often these quiet places have counters in them, behind which stand men who will serve you alcohol. Children don't like these places, and most of the time aren't welcome in them anyway.

Instead I have to spend most of my time in playgrounds and parks and zoos and indoor adventure arenas (large warehouse buildings covered in padding and netting through which children can maraud with little chance of damage to themselves). I don't like these places but my kids do, and I like to see them have fun. I also never enjoy being a hate figure in adult-centric situations.

Many parents like to bring their children, as early as possible, to museums and art galleries. Why? I wonder. The risk/reward ratio seems unfairly skewed in the risk area. There are so many things to damage, so many artistically inclined (generally intolerant) people to piss off. Much as I like to browse somewhere of intellectual importance, I'll do it when not being pestered to go to the café to buy jelly. Jelly and art—they belong in different spheres.

As a result there are two hurdles to overcome when negotiating the world with your upright child: your own desire to hang in places you enjoy; and your revulsion at spending valuable relaxation time in places filled with the sounds of screams and bright paint. You must forget both and forge ahead. The compromise is that your joy is now proportionately linked to theirs. In a place of your choosing, one where you feel comfortable, where you might experience a high percentage of happiness, say 75 per cent, the fact that they feel nothing but boredom means that your 75 must be multiplied by zero. Resulting in a score of zero and unhappiness all around.

If on the other hand you spend the afternoon encased in the tomb-like atmosphere of an emporium probably named NRG or FunZone, you may experience happiness levels of 25 per cent. The kids are knocking up in the 80s or 90s though, they're buzzing. Multiply that by your 25 and NRG wins every time. Prepare yourself for long afternoons being surrounded by children running and spinning after eating chocolate cake. Prepare yourself for kid hell.

Inevitably you get drawn into the mix in these places. A younger kid can be frightened by the sheer size and demonic quality of the places, older kids become bored as they gear up to start doing glue beyond the realms of your power. But between these two situations there is pure giddy mayhem to be enjoyed by most children. You can try to read a paper or a book, but that's difficult when you're being roared at every seven seconds, 'Look at me Daddy, look at me!' over and over again. The book defence is certainly important though, to protect you from random conversation with other parents.

You see, some parents see playgrounds and kid centres as an

opportunity to socialise. They have not grasped the compromise that you have made. You are here because to be anywhere else would result in blood being spilt, possibly yours, but more likely someone else's. They are here so the kids can have a run. But also on the off-chance they might meet someone they can talk to. About the kids, namely theirs. This type of person is obviously to be avoided at all costs and so the book can prove to be an important shield, especially if it has some academic relevance and you can intimate that you are studying. But again this is a risky technique because the supply of any type of information can provide an opening for further questioning, questioning that may start out about you but will quickly move on to them and then, unstoppably, on to their kids. Anybody that sees an adventure playground as a potential pick-up point for new buddies is more than likely a social leper. Even though your own social sphere has probably diminished since the growth of your own brood, you have no need to stoop this low. Read your book or paper, 'look' when commanded, pick the child from the floor after tumbles, supply copious amounts of money to be inserted into machines and handed over at the snack counter, and leave without any additional compadres. For your integration into society to work you have to step into a new society, but you don't have to buy a house there.

Being directed to places you wouldn't normally go is made worthwhile by the eureka moments. It's a cold, October evening and you're attempting to extricate them from the park. The only thing on your mind is getting them in the car, home, fed, bathed and asleep. Their aim is to stay out as long as possible. Just as your impatience starts to get the better of you, after numerous calls to get moving have been met with hilarity and dashes for cover, you come across your three-year-old daughter wrestling with a rotten log. Underneath, in the sodden earth, she spies ants, woodlice, worms and beetles, sprinting in panic from this grinning giant. She looks up at you in awe and you realise if things had gone smoothly you would have missed this.

FEEDING WITHOUT AN I.V. DRIP

I have friends whose kids rush to the table and vacuum their food. Their one-year-old daughter spoons down her porridge with a utensil that looks like a ladle in her chubby paw before banging her bowl on the table until it is refilled. These kids eat everything: stew, duck, couscous, moussaka, semolina, poached eggs and/or Flora margarine. Sometimes all together. Their meal times last approximately seven seconds, until the cupboards and plates are emptied of food. It is as if the room is suddenly filled with snarling hyenas where before there was the usual noise of general kid mayhem. I don't know how this happens, maybe their mother starves them for all but a half hour of each day, but it is a joy to behold. These kids love their food.

My kids eat nothing, nothing healthy anyway, at least not without a protracted negotiation. Where the aforementioned children turn feral at the prospect of mouldy cheese rinds, mine have to be cajoled into nibbling fillet steak prepared by a two-star Michelin chef. Their approximation of the canine species is to turn on the puppy dog charm for anything containing sugar or E numbers and then hit the thoroughbred sulks when their pleas are rejected. This is a prime example of parental paying slowly in the long term for short-term gratification when they were kids.

The baby books tell you to introduce a child to solids with vegetables before fruit, the reason being that once a child has a taste of sweet nectarine he will never be enthused by the less invigorating charms of the poor potato. I hear that and I understand it. But I am an idiot. So, when spoonfeeding a young child I chose to either cook or buy products that I wouldn't mind having a bit of myself, and I didn't fancy the carrot and parsnip mix. I did, however, enjoy the apple purée. Now I have larger kids who want to live on Mars bars and presume they are doing you a favour by eating two mouthfuls of the organic chicken you took out a second mortgage to buy.

I like to eat well and I like to eat a lot; so does the mother of our children. We cannot understand where their palates or appetites came from. Maybe the famine hunger died with our generation, but our kids have no inclination to either try new tastes or eat vast amounts. Unable to leave food behind, I clean their plates and have had to start running marathons to beat the expansion of my waist thanks to a serious scraps habit. This may sound like a minor concern, but the daily grind of coaxing food into a child has the same effect as water on rock. Slowly you are worn down until even approaching the family dinner table raises parental anxiety levels.

I see the mother taking a long time to prepare something nutritious and tasty, despite the fact that she has spent eight hours immersed in a job that taxes her after a night of broken sleep. She brings the meal to the table and we all sit, eventually, after hunting round the house to find children who insist we should bring food to them. The adults start to chew, the others start to manoeuvre. They push the food, knowing that we are waiting for them to make it disappear. They know what is required of them and are determined to defy us, and in their own way determine to distract us. They start by staring malevolently at each other. Kicking commences under the table. A morsel of chicken is thrown.

'Stop it. Eat your dinner.' One of us speaks.

'She started it. She kicked me.'

'She's making faces at me. She put up her bad finger.'

We distract, we coax, we encourage conversation, we play games. Eventually, after all ploys are exhausted, we attempt to spoon vital energy-giving foodstuffs into their closed mouths as they pick and choose when to open them. We do this knowing that they are capable of feeding themselves and they take some sort of perverse pleasure in us having to baby them. Usually we reach a point where we know they have consumed enough not to fade away during the night and we dismiss them. They commence the battle for ice-cream now, and sometimes they win and sometimes we have the strength to repel. Then I start my nightly crawl over the leftovers, too proud to let the congealed mess go in the bin.

This sounds miserable and is a little unfair. They do provide a confrontation most nights as to what they will digest, but occasionally they will surprise and sit and eat and chat contentedly. Even when they don't, their attempts at distraction and deception at the kitchen table are encouraging in their invention. Food is moved from plate to plate, placed in napkins, slipped onto the floor, thrown at us and each other. Drinks are spilt directly onto plates, rendering the pitch unplayable. Tantrums are manufactured to encourage removal from the table. Achievements are announced in attempts to negotiate rewards which can take the form of freedom from food. They are cunning and intelligent, and when operating in tandem can be quite effective.

The Bad Dad sits and wonders was it ever thus. He remembers his own family dinner table, where you got what you were given and, even if you weren't entirely thrilled, you didn't dare question either the quantity or the quality. You ate and you said thanks and you left. There may not have been riveting philosophical discourse at the table but you knew where you stood, and that was way down the totem pole. Now, when you should be sitting at the top of the table, sleeves rolled up after a long day's graft, responding to questions on the state of the nation, directing affairs, you are bent in supplication to a three-year-old in the hope that she'll swallow down another mouthful of carrot. The advancement of social equality has made a mockery of the gender wars. At the table at any rate, the kids are in control. We must rise up and take back our place. We must stand and demand that our bread and butter pudding be served to us first and that we be allowed to enjoy it in respectful peace!

THE LURE OF THE BEDSIT

As the kids get bigger they offer that much more scope for entertainment. They can respond to you and express what they want. Their characters become visible, they start to show who they will become. Back in the baby days you longed for this, for a time when they could ask you for something instead of screaming in frustration. You presumed it would be easy. But now they can ask, they can't stop asking.

At some point in the little big kid stage you realise that it's never going to get easy. You are woken up at 6.30 on a Saturday morning to turn on cartoons and supply bowls of cereal before returning to bed where you are treated to the rising sounds of discontent and fist on flesh in the room below. You realise that they will never be as delicate as they were when they first ambled along, but they will always have need of you and that need will for some inexplicable reason always have to be expressed when you are either in a deep sleep or about to nod off.

This realisation can be daunting. No matter how much you love them and take joy from them, knowing that they're not going to leave you alone until they head off to college and possibly for a lot longer can seriously rattle your cage. At the outset you measure the kid's life in weeks and then months and finally years. To begin with you advance through phases (feeding, teething, sleeping, toilet training) and as each one passes it seems that you're closer to the top of the hill. Then you look up ahead and there's no plateau in sight. That can make you tired.

It's then you might start to consider the bedsit. The thought of a room, 12 x 6, with a kitchenette that doubles as a bathroom, can appear appealing simply because it's quiet. Because there isn't enough room for anybody else to ask you to do things for them. Throw in a bottle of Buckfast and a regular supply of sleeping tablets and you have a viable alternative to family life. You can see yourself in a dirty mac, patrolling the streets on the scrounge for enough cash to buy a six pack of Dutch Gold, and instead of feeling revulsion or pity, for the first time you experience something like hope.

Attractive as that may be, at some point you might want to return to the fold and help clean up someone else's vomit other than your own. It's a difficult proposition for a partner to accept you back when you have consciously chosen to become a bum rather than a father. The kids may also resent you so this could be an option best left on the shelf.

PRESCRIPTION DRUGS AND THEIR ROLE IN THE MODERN FAMILY

One way to alleviate the need for cheap wine and life in a hostel is to indulge a small prescription drug habit. GPs are known to be more difficult to persuade to part with a script for anti-depressants and tranquillisers these days than in times past, but it's still about as difficult to get the goods as it is to club a baby for her wine gums. He may look at you disparagingly if you claim existential angst and non-specific anxiety or depression, but mention that you're losing the rag with the kids and you need to get the head down—he'll sort you with whatever you need.

Your drug problem could be alleviated and save you a course of rehab and possible loss of job by simply medicating the kids themselves. We are an organic family and as such I have had to smuggle Calpol onto the premises on occasion to earn a quiet night. There are many ways to treat ill health and unfortunately the general public has become aware that drug companies are not altruistic charities and are attempting to make money off our backs. As a result, while we are still inclined to gorge on painkillers to ease our own, often self-inflicted, suffering, giving medication to a child is seen as somewhere between a no-no and strictly a last resort in most middle-class, organic-wool-wearing households throughout the western world. This is a tough call because the benefits of kids' drugs are many, primarily the fact that they usually knock the blighters out. The fact that they might also cause them to develop gills and a gift for telekinesis are secondary when you consider how much more harmonious the family is when everyone has slept and nobody has a dry hacking cough. Extra-terrestrial growths can also be real conversation starters in the playground.

The beauty of your kids being denied regular meds is that when, finally, you succumb and throw some ibuprofen down their necks the effect is magnified as they have no tolerance to the stuff. They roll around the place like the junkie heroes of Irvine Welsh's seminal novel *Trainspotting*, which in itself is an advertisement for an alternative lifestyle to fatherhood. If you like, you could engage with the novel and nickname your offspring 'Renton', 'Sick Boy' and 'Begbie' and see if they develop their respective character's traits depending on the dosage you slip them.

But, essentially, drugs are a bad thing to develop a reliance on in your fathering plan, for yourself or the kids. Stick to love and respect and you may be able to avoid pouring heroin on their cornflakes down the line as they learn to question your every utterance. It plays havoc with their teeth and dentists cost a fortune.

Chapter 12

The Arrival of the Interloper

YOU ASKED FOR IT, YOU GOT IT

Just when everything was running smoothly, you're pregnant again. The 'you' in that sentence is plural but also used to highlight the fact that you (singular) are also very pregnant. The day after the birth of our second child I stopped by the local shop to tell the owner about the drama of the previous twenty-four hours. I happened to use the phrase 'We had a girl.'

A sour-faced pram pusher at the counter piped up, 'She had the baby, you had bleedin' nuthin to do wirrit.'

I was on such a high her comments barely registered, although they insinuated themselves over time because I had everything to do with it. You might get away with being an onlooker the first time round, but for every subsequent progeny you'll be expected to roll up the sleeves and muck in from the outset. And the outset is early.

This time round everything is different. Pregnancy is seen as an inconvenient path to delivery, and birth itself is expected to pass like a dental extraction. The reason for this is simple. You've both done this before and so are well prepared for the inevitable difficulties along the way. You have to abide by this principle as well, as for either of you to whinge or moan about the lack of attention being paid by the general population towards your latest development would smack of self-obsession. The world stops for you and your firstborn, it doesn't hesitate thereafter. This is a mantra you have to adopt once the pee-stick turns blue: this time you're on your own.

In what other area of expertise would you be expected to have a handle on proceedings after attempting them once before? If you got behind the wheel of a car and managed to move it round the block, who would advise you to head off now onto the nearest motorway? The only organisation I know of that operates like that is the Football Association of Ireland.

Poor old Steve Staunton grasped the Irish manager's job when offered, countering the claims of inexperience by citing his international record as a player, his close links to the professionals in the squad at that time, and his renowned determination. All of which counted for nothing when he went on to achieve some of the worst results ever managed by an Irish team. Cyprus, anyone? In much the same way, we all do this, mothers and fathers, when we go for more kids. 'Don't talk to me about being up the duff or forcing one out,' we say. 'We've been through it once before, sure aren't we experts?'

Pride and falls are integrally linked. Everything is just as hard the second time round, only you have to pretend it's a cakewalk. Everyone knows what you're going through and while some may sympathise, they don't have time to give you a digout. And this time you have the firstborn along for the ride.

PREGNANCY SECOND TIME OUT
The first trimester

Cast your mind back to watching *The Omen* for the first time. There are any number of scenes in that movie that build terror to the stage where you sense a tipping point and insanity beckoning. But there are two key factors involved and neither of them relate to gore, superstition or Catholic fear of the devil. First, the director, Richard Donner, paid as much attention to the development of suspense as he did to the delivery of blood and bone. Second, Donner made full advantage of the soundtrack *Ave Satani* by Jerry Goldsmith, increasing the operatic tempo at crucial points and introducing Latin chants during particularly suspenseful moments. The resulting movie is remembered worldwide as a chiller, something that makes you re-experience the way you felt the first time you watched it. It gets to you in a way that few other horror movies do, particularly those overly reliant on effects and bodycount.

Consider then the subsequent *Omen* movies. You may remember the occasional incident, but none of them instigate the experiential sensations that the first one does. They were cash-ins on success; they never really worked.

The first trimester of pregnancy as experienced by the father is a lot like the *Omen* movies. That is not to imply there is any sort of satanic intervention in your child's gestation, more to say that where the first event may have scared you to your marrow, the second will produce some uncomfortable moments but nothing shocking, providing, of course, everything goes to plan. Well, as close to plan as these things are ever wont to go.

The mother undergoes the same physical experience, of course. Again there is little in the way of outward development to suggest the machinations going on under the cover of her stomach but, thankfully, she doesn't seem to want to take out her discomfort quite as much on you. There is no guiding light from a first pregnancy as to whether she will experience morning sickness on this one. She may have had a clear run on her maiden voyage and be stricken on the second and, of course, the opposite may apply. Either way, her mental and physical states will have an effect on the joy of your life together, but the sharpness of their impact will be tempered by the presence of the existing child. You have to be aware and acknowledge what's going on inside; the kiddie cares not a jot. The kid's attitude is gold for you—Mother can't kick your ass with a witness in the house.

There is the downside to this. It would be foolhardy of you to risk adopting the playboy, churlish attitude discussed during this stage in Chapter 2. Nobody will forgive you for being an asshole when you have a child to take care of; everybody has to attempt to be a little mature about proceedings when you've been through them already.

The first trimester, so, is a time for reconciliation and a checking of boundaries. The physical symptoms have a mental impact. She feels the arrival of new life and lets you know about it. You begin to realise the implications of your ever so leisurely decision to increase the numbers. Yet neither of you can blow out, no matter how much you want to. Both of you become aware of how difficult it was to come to terms with the changing dynamic of your relationship with a birth and how, just as you had got your house in order, you've gone and upset the apple-cart again. She tries not to batter you and you try not to behave like a baby. The kid, meanwhile, the one on the outside, continues to bound along her path immune to the whole thing.

The second trimester

The beauty of T2 back then was, if you were lucky, a revamped sex life. A full, blooming, raunchy return to the playground of the early days when you were together. Once again her body begins to change in a way designed to get spirits soaring and loins yearning, but there is an extra set of beady eyes in the house to halt any impromptu acts of desire.

Fortunately, this time round you might not have so much to be sorry about after T1, providing you didn't fold like a gambler with deuces and go off the rails. It would be a pity not to be able to take advantage of the physical rewards of T2 due to morally deviant behaviour during the previous three months, so it would always be advisable to put in for some 'alone' time with your partner during these three, as time alone sure as shit won't be forthcoming when the nipper arrives. She, with the benefit of experience, is also painfully aware of what is to come and will, if a sympathetic human, wish to promote as much 'togetherness' as possible. You're getting ready to batten down the hatches: shag while you can.

The child will also become aware that Momma is getting porky and will have been told about the impending arrival. This usually results in great excitement but also a slow, creeping awareness that her place at the top of the heap may be under threat. You, being utterly and slavishly still beholden to your firstborn, will assure her that nothing could remove her from the crosshairs of your attention, but she may not believe you, considering you're spending every spare minute dragging Mammy upstairs where the bed shakes while she is left in front of Nickelodeon.

For the missus too, there will not be as great a softening and a return to humanity as before. Because she didn't hate you as much at the start, she may not like you as much in the middle, so make yourself charming for a change. Put in some work during T2 for your own sake as much as hers because by the time T3 rolls around, even though everything probably seems to be running relatively smoothly with your new-found maturity, all hell will still break loose. T1 and T2 are surprisingly different experiences from what you have previously known. T3 reminds you how history likes to repeat itself.

The third trimester

As the film poster for *Alien 3* proudly proclaimed, the bitch is back.

We are quite pathetic creatures, us men. Here is our wife/partner/lover, already a mother to a child of ours, struggling down the final stretch to give birth to another descendant, another glorious addition to the statistics books. She packs on the pounds, suffers varicose veins and haemorrhoids, can't eat what she likes and has cravings for all manner of things that are not only bad for her but probably bad for the atmosphere. She may be enduring this while struggling to work forty hours a week, continuing to do the shopping and providing a laundry service for you and your child. As she sweats around the place, determined to prove her Wonder Woman credentials, we get resentful because she occasionally responds snappily to our demands.

These are the facts: she gets pregnant, she balloons, she suffers the aches and pains of this massive growth, she experiences the excruciating pain of childbirth. We merely have to stand beside her along the way and occasionally offer support. On the second and following babies we must also acknowledge that she has entered into this process in the full knowledge of the difficulties she will encounter, and that we should be grateful for the steps she has taken to act as incubator for our unborn child. In our pathetic, snivelling, self-pitying states we then go on to complain about how difficult it is to cope with her moods during this difficult time. We should slap ourselves for being so weak. Those are the facts.

Except they are the facts as presented by the pregnancy public relations machine, the same machine that has every woman rolling her eyes at any problem a father may experience during pregnancy because, for Christ's sake, he can't possibly have anything to complain about compared to what she's going through. For him, as well, the bastard!

Maybe our concerns are pitiful. Maybe we shouldn't swan in after an afternoon on the links and expect to be lent a sympathetic ear for shooting over 100 as she approaches week 38 and has just spent the day entertaining six three-year-olds with story-telling, arts and crafts and music lessons. Maybe our headaches don't stand up to hers, maybe our stresses and anxieties pale in comparison to the fact that she has to cart her extra six stone up the stairs to the only toilet in the house every ten minutes because you never got round to installing a downstairs lav. Maybe we are a bunch of selfish, self-obsessed little boys.

But our woes are our woes. Just because the lady we wake beside happens to be going through what to her feels like the advance of doom does not detract from the fact that we still have our lives to lead. Pregnancy, and the third trimester in particular, gives rise to the belief in the superiority of woman. It is a peculiarly Catholic theory this, working along the lines of suffering expecting reward, of pain and discomfort as marks of virtue. Mmm, if I had a choice of being born German in the first half of the last century or American in the second half, I know I'd be chomping down on my slice of apple pie with a grin on my face. Suffering is to be avoided. Let her have her third trimester superiority and enjoy your golf.

THE JOY OF BIRTH SECOND TIME ROUND
They say it happens quicker second time round. Often they are right, but 'they' say a lot of things and not all of them should be attended to.

The beauty and the nightmare of the second birth is you know what's coming and so shouldn't fall into any of the pitfalls of first-time parent anxiety. She should have a better idea of how things are going approaching the delivery date. You both might have some thoughts on practical ways to get things moving should the need arise (see Chapter 3) and you'll probably choose not to go to the hospital until you actually need to.

The temptation of the home birth

I chose not to mention the possibility of a home birth in Chapter 3 simply because most people choose not to opt for this until at least the second birth. This is not cast in stone and I know of one woman who has had both her children, two joyous experiences, in the comfort of her own home. Well, it was actually her mother's home. She claims this was because the home-birthing service was not available in her own area, but I have a sneaking suspicion that she had the good sense not to get her own carpets and furniture ruined.

Raising the possibility of home birth induces serious reactions in people. Usually this comes in the form of: 'Are you fucking mental? There are no serious drugs in your house. Can the midwife or nurse bring heavyweight, charging rhino stopping drugs? Again, are you mental?'

The notion of having the child at home brings to mind Dickensian images and the usual pile of towels, jug of hot water and damsel in distress with misted forehead. The doctor arrives by horse-drawn carriage, surveys the playing field and sighs. Robust young men wait outside, wringing hands and smoking. Eventually a child's scream splits the air and there are hugs all round.

We don't generally want this in our house. Unless we're watching a Jane Austen costume drama on the Beeb on a Sunday night where home births are dramatic but fun, we have an engrained, conditioned response that babies should mark their arrival in the (usually) sterile environment of a hospital.

But there is the other response to the home birth suggestion: 'Oh my God, that is a cool idea. The baby will have such a relaxed birth experience, it will benefit his development and open his chakras to love and light.' You know who I'm talking about. She's a friend of your missus, she's done all the courses, she's possibly a Reiki master, and she certainly does not have any children. This hippy, policy-undermining stance is one to be guarded against. She will bend your missus's ear to the beauty of the occasion and draw pretty pictures in the air of oil-scented rooms and incense-heavy ambience. She will basically describe the interior of her regular masseuse's room, a wonderful place to go if you want to ease out the knots in your shoulders and listen to some whale music but not if you're having a baby. However, due to her charmed, calm exterior, possibly due to the ingestion of some potent weed (by the friend) over lunch, she will appear particularly appealing to your missus and may cause mental cogs to be turned, guiding her to the birthing pool.

The next thing you're being introduced to a home-birth midwife who just happened to be passing and is sitting waiting to answer any of your queries. She has obviously been briefed on your concerns and is ready and willing to patronise you out of them.

First off she will speak about how the home is the most natural place in the world for a woman to give birth. She will talk about bears and rabbits retreating to their caves with their newborns and getting to know their litter in the dark, cosy atmosphere of their own den. She will highlight how wonderful it will be for the mother and the child to experience birth in their own domain and to move afterwards into the maternal bed, the 'den' as it were. She will make it sound like trying on a new, warm pair of 100 per cent lambswool slippers.

She will then get serious and move on to issues of health which she knows you are extremely concerned about. She will assure you that every prospective father is concerned about the well-being of the people most important to him in the world, and the fact that you are concerned marks you out as a particularly sympathetic husband and dad. When it comes to the delivery, obviously your concerns are heightened but what you have to realise is that the home is actually the safest place for this event to take place. She will mention in passing that many people pick up bugs while in hospital, as do babies, and a surprisingly high number of people die while there. She won't mention these things to disparage the health system and promote herself, she's just mentioning them in passing, y'know. At this stage you might want to place a slice of toast under her chin to catch the honey dripping out. You, she will tell you, as a father should be concerned for the safety of mother and child during birth—particularly if it is happening in a hospital.

She does not have access to pain medication but if you choose to use a pool, it will provide a great deal of relief. In the highly unlikely incident of there being complications you are only a short drive away from the hospital or an ambulance could get to the house within minutes. Of course, that won't be necessary but she acknowledges you are concerned and you need to prepare for every eventuality—that's your job. You are the big, strong dad.

So, you have scented candles burning, love and peace in the air, a plunge pool in your living room, the prospect of a birth you can invite friends to as it's going to be so easy you may as well make a night of it. By the time she's finished speaking you're nodding along with her and both you and the missus are grinning like you've just won the speedboat on *Bullseye*.

This is why you never let door-to-door double glazing salesmen across the threshold. Because of their silver tongues and your inability to say no. You're talking about turning your living room into a jacuzzi populated by one woman who is bound to lose control of her sphincter. You will never again be able to relax on your leather couch, dip Doritos and watch *Football Focus* without thinking about what you once had to wipe off the seats.

The problem is, most of what the midwife says is true. It's just that those who opt for home births tend to be baby-dropping mamas with hips the width of the Khyber Pass and Wonder Seed Dads. For dad in particular, it is an opportunity to once again show how easy this birthing lark is. If these people could, they would strap a birthing pool to a rollercoaster in Alton Towers and get on with things mid-loop the loop. They could give birth in line at the till in Tesco and not notice until the baby was scanned and the girl calling for a price check. As a result both the figures and the anecdotal evidence are skewed. Most normal people realise there may be trouble ahead, hopefully not but there is a possibility, and want to be somewhere that contains lots of people with qualifications and access to narcotics. It makes sense.

THE ACTUAL BIRTH

I can't imagine witnessing the birth of your child can ever become mundane. As a physical act, it is fraught with danger and potential complications, which all contribute to the intensity of the emotion when the thing is completed. The beauty of birth is that, while nothing can prepare you for the emotion of meeting your child, the same experience washes over you again the next time out. Once again you are thrown into the front line, once again you witness the mother endure what seems impossible pain, once again you are utterly useless and in the way of anyone who is there to help. Once again you are overwhelmed with love for mother and baby. You can't beat that, you can't bottle it, you can't buy it, however often it happens.

WHY DOES NO-ONE CARE THIS TIME ROUND?

It's when you get back to the ward or the room after the baby has been born that a realisation dawns on you. Most likely you will be joined by the other little blighter, and how she responds to her new sibling will be an interesting process to witness unfolding, but what slowly becomes apparent is that you're on your own.

Okay, some people will drop in. You'll have grandparents bopping round the place, your brothers and sisters, family mainly —if they can make it. But there are no trumpets and fanfare, the arrival isn't heralded as if it's the first child to have ever made this perilous journey and, because that is what you had last time, you might feel a little hurt. First time round the room was so festooned with flowers and champagne they were holding AA meetings in the next ward and had allergy notices at the entrance. You had acquaintances last seen in primary school appear at the bedside and people making long-haul last-minute flights to wet the baby's head. Now you've got your close family, the ones you see most weeks. The ones who count, it's just you're not counting now because you're pissed off and want a bit of attention. Ya big baby.

Of course people care, they just don't care a whole lot. They're busy too. The delivery ward realisation is important because it's an indicator of how things are going to go when you get home. Not so many visitors for this one, not so many gifts, fewer baby clothes and you can forget about cash. Paradoxical as it is, you have twice the amount of work and you can be sure less than half the offers of help. This baby is coming into a working house with no pretensions (maybe aspirations to) of grandeur. It'll have to start to pull its weight soon enough and never develop the monarchical demeanour that the elder one surely has.

People don't care, not because they don't care, but because they didn't really want to wish you all that well for the first one. There's a maniacal atmosphere in the air surrounding the birth of a first child. Old friends crawl out of the woodwork because they know you've gone, you've turned to the dark side, the one smeared with baby vom and crap, and they're unlikely to see you again for a long time. First time out marks the end of an era and the start of a new one, and everyone wants to see people in the process of change, as they embark naively and smiling into the nether world of new baby maintenance.

Second time round, they know you're doomed already. They know if they come to see you they'll be regaled with tales of labour and bursting perineums but they'll see in your eyes the resignation at what you're facing into. There's no craic in watching a bubble deflate, it's all in the bursting. Everyone still wants to wish you well, but not so many come because there's no value for money in the visit.

WHEN ELDER KIDS ATTACK: WITNESSING FRATRICIDE
'Whenever possible, don't get involved.'[9]

There's very little parenting advice you get from websites or in books that you wouldn't already know if you had time to sit and assess a situation in peace without a child screaming at you. We tend to only seek advice when there is drama which usually involves conflict and our own heightened mood. At that point we'll clutch at anything. The little nugget on the previous page comes from the kidshealth.org website and it floats my boat.

I would apply that piece of advice to most kid situations, particularly ones where a referee is being asked for or an intervention is required. If at all possible, let someone else do it. However, on this site that tip is given as information which can then be supplied as your strategy in dealing with sibling rivalry. 'I'm doing nothing because the website told me so. Mine is a valid approach. I don't care if one of them has just stabbed the other, I'm following instructions.'

Of course, this approach is followed with the proviso that you encourage the kids to sort out their difficulties together. This kind of passive approach generally involves more work than the old-school bellow, 'Leave your brother/sister alone or I'll batter ye!' which still applies in many quarters. You'd be surprised how often this disciplinarian technique is still used.

A friend recently informed me of hearing the following piece of parenting genius issued on his street. Mother to three-year-old son: 'Get in for your dinner now, ye little prick, or I'll dance on yer face.' The way the order was both issued and received implied that this was a perfectly normal way of communicating in that family. In that spectrum of behaviour, I think the ability to stand back from problematic situations would be seen as high-performance parenting.

When child number two comes home, one of the first things to occur will be child number one's attempt to kill her new sibling. This will be done with a genial smile on her face, possibly in full view of a houseful of visitors cooing, 'Do you love your new brother?' or 'Isn't your little sister great?' She can't stand the new arrival and she can't say that, only her murderous actions reveal her inner thoughts. So starts eighteen years of love/hate rivalry.

You are coping with a new baby, with doing all the typical demands new baby brings, while the other child decides she wants your full attention right bloody now. Of course you can't give it, and neither can Mum, and for the first time first child realises she isn't quite the hero she thought she was. You are to blame, Mother is to blame, but you're both too big to give a proper kicking to. Now where's my hammer and where's that baby. Let's see if she can take one to the head.

It's all quite stressful, but it's funny at the same time, witnessing the overtly underhand attempts to hug and choke a child while you look on. You have one priority, that both of them survive. One is in danger from the other, while the other is in danger from you, should you lose the rag. Get out of the house for walks and take the older brat with you. Remind her you still think she's okay and you're not going to send her to the workhouse just because another has arrived on the scene. But threaten that you just might have to pack her off if you catch her near the crib with a carving knife again. Then go and have a pint and try and forget about it all.

RESISTING INFANTICIDE

The elder child may well be under threat from you for reasons that you could claim temporary insanity for down the line, but the new arrival will also push buttons that the first one never did. Think about it; for baby one, both sets of grannies put down their knitting needles and gardening gloves and fought over who got to help more. You couldn't turn a corner in your house for a month without a cup of tea being put in your hand and instructions being issued for you to sit and take a rest.

You had no real handle on the financial implications because back then your parents were arguing over who'd get to pay for nappies and babygros and sterilisers and you were sleeping on a bed of soft sleepsuits from babyGap that had been provided as gifts. After a month you were possibly quids in and becoming accustomed to the bacon sandwich handed to you by your mother-in-law as you stepped into the kitchen each morning.

None of that happens on the second. She is clothed in hand-me-downs and your house echoes to the sound of only your own voices, and sometimes your quiet sobbing. The grannies phone daily but they have had their baby fix and are comforting themselves with knitting christening gowns and growing tomatoes. The grandads wink knowingly at you on their way out for a day in the bookies or as they get their boat's rigging in order. Occasionally they'll slip you a bottle of wine for succour.

Yes, this time you're really on your own. You're a little bit older and may not have ever got back into a decent sleep routine since the birth of the first child. When the baby wakes in the middle of the night you do your thing and walk the floors, but often first child is envious and will get up too and demand you make porridge. The tiredness you experienced first time round, which felt like a term in Abu Ghraib, is eclipsed by the fatigue of number two and nobody else cares. You become rather ratty.

Every time somebody utters the words, 'Listen mate, it'll pass' you feel like garrotting them with their own tie, knotted perfectly because they have time to concern themselves with such things. You know it'll pass, you just don't think it'll pass quick enough.

The kids are still as gorgeous as ever. You begin to realise how easy it is to get on with your toddler because she can tell you what she wants or doesn't want. She likes to demonstrate her needs in the most dramatic way possible, but that's easier to fathom than the re-immersion in the new baby cacophony as they come to terms with the world. Having said that, the new one also reminds you how quickly they change and how you don't notice these changes as time passes, not until you are brought back to the start again. When you remind yourself of these things, you start to enjoy yourself.

BATTENING DOWN THE HATCHES

The reason you don't get so much attention this time round is not only because people can't get as much fun out of witnessing you tumbling into the pit as was the case last time. Now there are four of you, you're your own little team. All right, just because you've done something once before doesn't make you an expert and you would appreciate some help (and cash never goes amiss), but you're not shocked by the time it takes to wash vests or sterilise bottles. The volume of work increases but you have learned skills that allow you to get through it on autopilot.

Acclimatising to number two reminds me of the great European explorers struggling through the Doldrums on their way to whatever new place they could find. Picture Columbus or Magellan without a clue as to what's in front of them but knowing there's no way back. Their crew is beset with scurvy and semi-psychotic, their water is foul, there isn't a puff of wind and birds circle overhead. The only thing keeping spirits up is the possibility of a tryst with a Tahitian native at some point. That's your family for the first couple of months, and you're Christopher or Ferdinand, except without the final glory, wealth or recognition.

You keep a tight ship, you put the head down and make sure everyone knows what they're doing and nobody is intent on destroying anyone else. It's an extraordinary time as you enter a kind of combat mode. Until now there were a number of individuals involved, but with the growth from one child to however many, the collective mind comes to the fore and a unit is formed. All the usual crap has to be taken care of, money still has to be earned and everyone must eat, but, for a while, things are quiet as you take care of everyone's needs without a thought for the outside world. It can be frustrating and tiring and boring, but it needs to be done and, if I can run the risk of getting a smack in the mouth, it passes.

Soon enough everyone knows their new role. The nippers are set to wind each other up forever but the time when there was only one of them is soon forgotten, replaced with an acceptance that each needs to be looked after, or kept in her box, whichever school of thought you intend on subscribing to. The more that join them, the more streamlined the process gets, each time getting somewhat harder but not proportionately so. If you and Momma can still look each other in the eye during and after all this it's probably because you've learned to operate as a team without harbouring too much resentment.

Resentment for what you put in will, of course, kill a family. However, there is a slim line between monitoring your input and becoming resentful for what you do. You have to keep track of what's going on simply for the purpose of having some ammunition to bring to negotiations when you both emerge from the Doldrums and decide you want to engage with the world again. Acknowledge each other's brilliance, but make sure your endeavours are recognised when arranging to start temporary visas from the nest.

Chapter 13

To Your Good Health

FOOD AND DRINK

There was a time, not so many years ago, when eating was something you did when you were hungry. Nobody does anything as simple as that any more. Your eleven o'clock snack isn't complete if it doesn't include taramasalata, what's a lunch if there's no ballotine of cured organic salmon, and dinner isn't dinner without veal sweetbread slowly caramelised and glazed with liquorice sauce.[10] Baked beans on toast in front of *EastEnders* you say? Peasant.

Eating and drinking in the twenty-first century is a competitive sport. It used to be an indicator of your rearing whether you knew your way around table settings at a formal dinner table, but now that is taken as a matter of course. Now you also need to be familiar with a number of world cuisines and respective utensils, know when using your hands is appropriate, know what's hot and what's not and why, and be emotionally involved with the plight of the poor creatures you're scoffing with such gusto at phenomenal prices. That's before you choose a wine.

Wine is the ultimate blagger's stage. Knowing your wines still retains an element of old world gentility, but get found out and you are the buffoon of the table. You bluff at your peril—propose yourself as a connoisseur only if you're on steady ground or if surrounded by drunken KFC regulars.

It's pathetic really. We pay through the nose for average food and occasionally find the sublime in a bacon sarnie down the local greasy spoon. Often the most comfort is to be found in the things we know, the shepherd's pie your mother makes or the bangers and mash you whip up yourself. But still we insist on launching into the *frissons* and the *jus de* stuff.

It's the same feeding kids. They like some gear and if you happen on a vein of something nutritious they will munch it continuously for a period. Scrambled egg for breakfast, poached for lunch and fried for dinner. You may have a three-year-old with the cholesterol of a two-time cardiac patient but they'll be full.

I have a theory that every parent buys peace at home by serving chocolate and ice-cream for each meal. But whenever a visitor enters the house there is a display of puréeing and dicing and chopping that would have Delia getting frisky. All the organic produce is rolled out, chicken that cost the GNP of a Pacific island nation, polenta, sweet potato and chickpea, with a starter of consommé and home-made cobbler for dessert. Because if eating out is serious among adults, cooking for kids is every parent's opportunity to demonstrate a level of sensitivity and panache heretofore never granted a stage.

Your baby starts on breast milk and then moves to mashed organic vegetables followed by fruit (has to be in that order—fruit first will spoil taste buds and they'll never touch a spud) and eventually organic, prime cuts of meat. Nothing that hasn't been tracked and autographed by the animal pre-slaughter passes the special one's lips. You refuse to consider anything in a jar or pre-cooked—you show you care by doing it yourself, and, besides, convenience is the invention of the devil.

Arse. Arsery I say. Give the kids enough tucker to provide them with enough energy to get them through the day without showing overt symptoms of malnutrition or scurvy. You've better things to be doing with your time than carving potatoes into animal shapes because that's the only way little Phedhlim will eat them. Give 'em porridge for breakfast, beans for lunch and meat for dinner. If they want chocolate or ice-cream give them some. Don't let them bathe in the shit and keep them moving. Kick ball, it'll burn calories and keep pizza in front of Playstation to a minimum. Kids don't give a shit about food, it's fuel between running from one dangerous scenario to the next. We're the ones who make it an issue, and we are dumbasses.

YOUR HEALTH AND THEIRS

How you cope with your child's health isn't so much competitive as top secret. Some mothers regard a weekly trip to the GP as par for the course and others won't let a doctor look in their child's ear until said child has coughed up a lung. I say mothers because when it comes to health, we're not involved: we know squat and our input would probably cause malaria or typhus at the very least. Maternal instinct rises and Momma becomes lioness when cub gets ill. One would have to be very qualified or very stupid to attempt to get between mother and sick cub.

With a child's health at stake, receive your orders from Mother on what to administer and when, should you be required, and watch how the lioness deals with other females in the pride. Mothers will ask each other how they treat their children but unless they are absolutely certain they are speaking to someone from the same school of thought (be that kill everything with codeine or treat bugs as a friend with homeopathy) they will be reluctant to reveal their approaches. Because if one mother's tack differs from the other, no matter how many times she says 'Well, I would do that differently but good luck to you and what's important is he gets better,' what it is obvious she is really saying is, 'Jesus, you're a shit mother, your kid's gonna die, you should be in jail and you're probably a junkie and a whore to boot.' That's what one mother hears the other say. You cannot comment on how a mother treats her sick child—that's breaking all the rules.

Doctors are forever complaining that men don't go for regular check-ups, that serious illnesses could be diagnosed much earlier if men presented with initial symptoms. But that's patently silly because we know if you ignore something for long enough it'll eventually go away. We go so far as to conduct all our relationships in the same manner until one woman refuses to leave.

It's probably best to engender the same approach in your kids. We know that scabs are there to be picked, itches to be scratched and weeping sores to be covered with plasters. Eventually, when the pain means you can't breathe any more, you pay a visit to the doctor, who will admonish you, perform a painful procedure and insist you come sooner next time. As if you would with that kind of reception to be expected. When your kids hurt themselves or pronounce themselves ill, bandage them and give them enough legal drugs to send them to sleep. Then wait until the lioness is available to inspect the damage. Never venture to casualty without approval, even if a bone is protruding through skin, or you will be blamed for the injury yourself. If there is no way of getting the mother to check things out, have a neighbour take a picture of the injury and sign a sworn statement that you had nothing to do with it. For the sake of your own health as well as theirs, try to keep the kids in reasonable nick and leave all major decisions to someone else. Your role is similar to that of the mafia's *consiglieri*, you can advise but don't ever expect to step up to the big chair.

THE DOCTOR

Your relationship with your doctor changes in odd ways when you move from being just a patient to both a patient and the father of another one. Grown men are typically viewed as buffoons by their GP. These are men who could make vital decisions in their working day, decisions that affect the bottom line of companies they represent, their own lifestyles and the living standards of those they are responsible for. These men eat stress, and they acknowledge in the course of every working day that when a problem arises it needs to be dealt with early and efficiently. These same men will tend not to go to the doctor unless a body part falls off.

As a result a doctor usually speaks to men the same way as we speak to our pre-school children. We resent him a bit for this, but we understand why he does it. He treats us like idiots because we behave like idiots when taking care of ourselves. He also knows that we tend not to go to the doctor, not because of a desire to live recklessly, but because we're afraid of what might be done to us there or what we might be told. In essence, we're cowardly about our own health mainly due to wanting to believe we're strong enough to ward off most illnesses. We also hate needles and know that at some point someone is going to want to put a hand in our bum and explore our prostate gland. This is one treat that can wait.

Our relationship and the concurrent dynamics have developed over the years. But when you start arriving in with a child, the doctor suddenly decides to give you regular bollockings. Has the child had its vaccinations, are you ensuring there are vegetables in the child's diet, are you keeping the child warm and clean? The sort of things that you would presume other people would presume you would do as a matter of course. Except the doctor knows you, and knows how careless you are when it comes to matters of health. So, it could be fair to say that the low rate of infant mortality is indirectly attributable to doctors having the sense to jump on fathers about the responsibilities that most people expect them to be aware of. When he gives the kid a lolly at the end of a visit, don't be shocked when he gives you one too.

THE DENTIST

Fear of the dentist is like licking the lid of a yoghurt carton— nobody tells you to do it, you just know. Dentists need a good makeover by a decent PR and advertising company because no matter how swish and painless they get they can't shake the medieval image of a blacksmith in a leather apron wrenching bloody molars from a drunken, tooth-ached wreck of a man. A lot of it is their own fault.

The only time I feel pain at the dentist is when he's cleaning my teeth and that's because he dictates this procedure does not require anaesthesia. If I'm getting anything else done he loads me up so nicely that I can get lost in Sky News conveniently dangling above my head as he ties knots in the veins running through my rotting gums. He's a genius, and the bastard's good-looking.

The problem is his clinic looks like it's been hewn from a centre spread in *Architecture Monthly*, his theatre sparkles like the bling on a gangsta rapper's fist (which I am thankful for) and his fees mount like a stallion on a fit filly. He's stinking rich because I need to know I go to the best because of my terror at one of those gleaming instruments scraping across a live nerve. Laurence

Olivier and Dustin Hoffman have a lot to answer for.

My relationship with my dentist is much more business-like than the one with my doctor. I know he's riding me and he knows I'm not going anywhere else because I revere him. I bring the kids along and he smiles because he can see the cheques rolling in for a whole generation. I have heard of some dumbass dentists who berate mothers for allowing their children to drink fizzy drinks resulting in cavities and a sugar addiction. The mothers, guilty at their negligence and angry at the inference, immediately make an appointment in another clinic. My fella looks in a child's mouth and assures me and them that he can cope with anything they throw at him. And they won't feel a thing. They walk out of there feeling like they've had a visit to a theme park crossed with a five-star hotel and look forward to going back. I'm relieved their teeth are in good hands and make a note to sell a kidney on the black market when the downturn for live organs changes.

He knows I fight with the kids about what sweets they can eat so he doesn't hint that I am responsible for decay in any way. He knows they usually win the fight because they can whine for longer than I can resist, and as a result he knows that we will always need him and for probably more than regular check-ups. He knows that anyone who spends their working lives staring down the throats of random, halitosis-suffering, toffee-chewing punters should be rewarded in this life and he knows that he has the keys to the bank vault. Because he can make the pain go away. I would personally pay for his new Mercedes CL (instead of part-paying for it as I already do) if he could guarantee that I and all of mine need never suffer toothache again. And he pretty much does. And he's good-looking. The bastard.

HEALTH RIVALRY AMONG FRIENDS

It's one thing to comment to a stranger or a mere acquaintance that you have a differing approach to healthcare than theirs when it comes to the kids. This will automatically halt any opportunity to develop a friendship, of course, but you don't care because you don't really know the person. You would think it would be different when conversing about the variety of ways to deal with illness with friends, but you would be wrong. Nothing inspires hatred where before there had been love like a comment on a fellow parent's part in a child's illness.

You'll find the occasional mum who still smokes through pregnancy. At this stage, having been shunted out into the wide open spaces to indulge their habit, just continuing to smoke at all marks a smoker's determination to maintain their daily quota. If regular smokers are society's pariahs, pregnant smokers are viewed with a disdain usually reserved for war criminals with a record of necrophilia. To continue to smoke in the face of insurmountable evidence that you are doing both yourself and your unborn child harm while the world spits bile at you requires a combination of stupidity, stubbornness and a certain bravery. Yet some mothers do it, and they'll generally combine their habit with a steady flow of red wine to keep their blood pressure down. Or beer, gin, vodka or Smirnoff Ice if there's no wine available.

We've all heard how our own mothers chewed their way through forty Players a day while up the stick with us and we turned out fine. But chucking out that argument nowadays is an attempt to flatten the world again. The mum smokes on and finally gives birth. She'll usually manage the delivery without a tab but of that you can't be certain, you'll see any number of expectant mothers chuffing at the entrance to maternity hospitals in their dressing gowns and I suppose some of them must be in labour. Anyway, the baby crawls spluttering into the world and immediately starts to skin up but is generally regarded as fine. Then the fun starts and no matter how ill that child ever gets, nobody can ever suggest that the problems might be linked to its mother loving her fags during pregnancy.

The child is born underweight—sure everyone on the mother's side was small when they were born. What's that got to do with anything? You suggesting something? Note the rising of the hackles.

The child could be hit by six chest infections in the first six months—it wasn't me Guv, the dad is asthmatic. Blame him for the weak lungs. In fact, so sure are the parents that asthma is inevitable they'll start the kid on inhalers, nebulisers and oxygen tents in advance. All down to weak lungs, y'know, better to be safe than sorry, genetic y'know, nothing we could do about it.

Next thing the kid's having kidney infections and stomach problems. Everyone rallies round to help the parents who are terrified and spending every waking moment in the hospital. Nobody wants this. Nobody mentions the smoking.

This is a very obvious example of how carefully we tread around other people and their behaviours linked to their kids' well-being. That mother should have had some sense slapped into her but nobody would dare to do it because of the code of silent commentary on child-rearing. Each of us worries for our children and we tend to be harsher on our own attempts than anyone else could ever possibly be. We know how hard parenting is and so are loathe to risk the wrath of a mother to stick our oar in on some inconsequential topic. The payback is that nobody comments on our often botched attempts. The downside is people still get away with justifying absolute lunacy, often as they reach for their ciggies resting on top of their bump.

Out here on the western outcrop of Europe we're a highly sensitive bunch. We can fight for our rights and promote ourselves as free thinkers and libertarians but we will not tolerate any external comment on our lifestyles, lifestyles which aren't much to shout about. In an over-inflated economy we work long hours to pay for over-priced houses, two new cars per household and sixty hours of childcare a week. That's not smart, that's stupid. We're tired and our kids barely know us, and when we get to spend two weeks in Cyprus each summer we make sure the nanny comes along because there's no way we could hack all that time with the kids hanging out of us. At some point we will have to step back and check if we're enjoying the lives we're carving out for ourselves and our families. But until this reluctance to comment on how we raise our families is addressed there is no way we can seriously consider adjusting the approach commonly taken as normal. And nowhere is this hypersensitivity more obvious than in attitudes towards medicine.

Whether we subscribe to the standard medical model or choose an alternative path, every parent has a similar motive and that's to keep their child well. Unless we can be open and inquisitive about the wealth of diverse opportunities out there we'll never be in a position to share both our acquired knowledge through experience and also take advantage of others' experience that's on our own doorsteps. At some point we have to raise the curtain on the family and share what's going on; a good swig of cough bottle might be a good place to start.

Chapter 14

Four to School

LIGHT AT THE END OF THE TUNNEL

One morning someone will ask you, 'So where are you sending her to school?' and you'll realise this isn't another drone question from an obsessive compulsive parent who had her kids' names down for the local Gaelscoil before they were conceived. It's quite possibly March, and your child is four, and she'll need to be getting some education in September. You'll have to give it some thought.

Your first thought might be that she can't be old enough for school, she's not ready. Then you realise she's been filing your end of year returns for the past eighteen months. But she won't be able to hack the playground bullies. Come on, the mortgage is half paid by the protection money she's pulling in from the kids on the avenue, no fears there.

In this cliché-ridden parenting world, they grow up so quick. One minute they're in nappies, happily pissing in your eye at every opportunity, and the next they're joy-riding in your new coupé. It feels like only yesterday you were forking out for a buggy and now here you are saving for her tongue-piercing and first tattoo combo in the local needle shop. Some parents lament this, but those parents are off their flaming trollies. She's going to school in six months: for a few hours every day she will be someone else's responsibility. From now on when she exhibits traits that could get her into strife with society you can blame either her teacher or her classmates. This is your get out of jail free card.

Having said that, this is the first milestone when what has, until now, been your private property enters the public domain. There will be certain concerns to be addressed for both parents and child, predominantly to do with how she will socialise with her new friends. Any overtly sociopathic tendencies exhibited in the first few days will be an indicator of how things roll in your house and you don't want your dirty laundry waving in the playground breeze. You also have to pry your fingers from the wheel of total control and let her new teacher begin to exert some influence.

You may have had experience of at least some level of childcare to this point, but there is a complete difference in how you address what goes on with the kid in school and what goes on in the crèche. With a babyminder, you lay down the rules, you enforce your philosophy and expect them to follow it. The school will tell you to stick that attitude in your pipe; when your kid crosses the threshold, the school owns them. Like a marriage, for better or for worse.

The end of the tunnel is in sight, but just beyond that you can see another tunnel and you recognise it as the fourteen years of obligatory education you endured yourself. Chucking her blithely into the waiting arms of the education system is a physical mark of the end of the baby years, and a reminder of the magnitude of the step she is taking. Nobody forgets their school days, so we should probably at least pay a little attention to the institution we choose to school them in.

CHOOSING A GOOD SCHOOL, I.E. THE ONE CLOSEST TO YOU THAT PROVIDES AFTERCARE

I have a problem with primary school—it just seems like playtime until they go to secondary school and have to learn something. I know this is all wrong and that if they haven't got the basics nailed down before they take off to the big place, well they're pretty much in the shits. But I can't get my head around taking the problem of where they should be sent for the first few years too seriously. As long as there are half decent sports facilities, less than the population of New Delhi in the class, a challenging jungle gym in the yard and the teacher wears a smile, then I'm happy. It also helps if the other kids don't march through the gates armed. That, I think, sends out a bad message.

Up at the crèche, for the two years before departure date, you'll have had mothers milling around concerned at where little Ashley or Ralph is going to cut his teeth. 'Pius's has wonderful IT infrastructure and they get them into the language lab from first class.' 'I'm not keen on the religious emphasis in St Mary's, but having said that they have done very well in the city leagues at football over the last few years. That shows commendable team spirit.' 'I'm having all my kids educated *as Gaeilge*, it's incredibly hard to get into the Irish school these days but Pronsias and Radharc have had their names down since birth, and, well, their dad's a friend of the Principal, y'know like. I mean "Ta fhios agat" hahaha!'

Then the dads show up and are sucked into the discussion. One will look at another and ask, 'So, where are you sending him then?'

'Dunno, she hasn't told me yet.'

'Give a shit?'

'Not really. As long as he plays a bit of ball and can read at the end of it, that'll do me.'

If you haven't morphed into everything you hated about your own parents as a teenager already, choosing a school and engaging in the reasons why will get you there. It's impossible not to sound like a prick doing it. You have the Ying and Yang act between parents, one coming over all Miss Jean Brodie and the other full of swagger and bullshit, the two combining to add to the fraud of making it a difficult choice.

Years ago you went to the school down the road and got a clattering from the Brothers or psychological annihilation from the nuns. Rightly enough, the traditional Catholic educational ethos that 'The beatings will continue until morale improves' was adjusted, but the national schools have been fighting an uphill public relations battle ever since corporal punishment was outlawed in the eighties. Alternative options have developed since but the national, State-sponsored, Catholic-driven school still dominates the landscape. And the problem is the Church has for the most part taken a belligerent stance in its role in education in Ireland.

Immigration has resulted in an increase in numbers of school-going children. With the variety of cultures and faiths entering the country and the continuing decline of religious practice in the typical Irish family, the openings available for people to have their children educated do not match their requirements. More than nine out of ten primary schools are national schools with a Catholic ethos. Most people are willing to overlook this for the sake of convenience but some take umbrage, seek alternatives and find there are none. In occasional cases children have been refused entry unless baptised. The Church's line on this is that if you are not Catholic you have no right to expect a place in its system. But there is no other option in many places because they've wrapped the system up in a greater monopoly than McDonald's could dream of and the government has no interest in regulating the problem.

So, at the outset there is a conflict, which is only exacerbated when we as parents get on our cloaks of preciousness and begin to pontificate on the importance of little Jane/Jonny 'getting the best start possible'. The reality is that it has little to do with where the monster goes to school, and a whole lot more to do with us showing how we are the most fantastic parents on the block and that we will go to the ends of the earth to ensure the child fulfils her potential and lives her (our) dream.

The sad fact is that our national school system is in general excellent where it's not dominated by hyper-vigilant Sister Agathas harking back to the glory days of the Magdalen Laundries. If the spotlight could be taken off who runs them and how, it would become more obvious that the job done in these schools is as good as anywhere on the planet. The brats go off to school and I, for one, want them to have a good time. I've been sat down with teacher at parent meetings and we've gone through the first child's reading, writing and maths skills and all I'm interested in is how she's mingling and enjoying the experience. I'm fortunate, and with typical parental arrogance, will state that I know she's bright. If she's to fall off the educational wheel it won't be because she can't handle a theorem or the Renaissance, it'll be because she's lost interest for some reason. And I expect her teacher to keep her lively and to help her embrace the time with her classmates and engage in what she's learning. They don't need a laptop and broadband at each desk for that, they need a creative teacher.

To that end I'm an odd mix of Machiavellian and stupid lazy in my choice of school. I have no time for or interest in religion in the education system, yet I will milk that system to its maximum and jump through whatever hoops required to ensure we get to have as much choice as possible. But the key and crucial point is that our local national school is around the corner; all else diminishes in importance compared to that extra few minutes in bed.

THE RISE OF THE GAELSCOIL/EDUCATE TOGETHER/NON-DENOMINATIONAL LOVE-IN

Antagonism towards the State school service has had some effect in that there has been a small rise in alternatives available. There were always private options if you were super concerned about the right accent and networking from an early age, but the kids who attend such schools are so routinely bullied for their lamentable blazers and so immersed in the 'honour' system that they wind up not knowing if they're Irish or on sabbatical here from a mid-twentieth century Enid Blyton novel. Also they may be forced to play cricket, hockey and tennis and never learn the tribal system of GAA culture.

Twenty years ago you sent your child to a Gaelscoil only if you could provide documentation that a relative of yours had shot at least six Black and Tans, if you spoke Irish at home with a Connemara accent even if you'd never lived beyond the confines of the South and North Circular Roads, or if you had an immediate member of the family running in local elections for Sinn Féin. Pupils at these schools were obliged to cheer whenever the Republican Army scored points in the Troubles and were also under orders to assault any member of the general public who dared to suggest that the violence in the North was attributable to acts of terrorism rather than acts of war. Parental political beliefs would trickle down into kids' psyches and there were many pitched street battles between bodhrán-wielding six-year-olds and their

Garret FitzGerald supporting counterparts, hurleys versus hockey sticks so to speak.

Nowadays those former Garret-loving urchins are parents to children whose presence is keeping the next generation of Shinners out of their beloved Gaelscoils. You are nothing in Dublin 6 and Dublin 4 if Sadhbh and Ruadhán can't converse fluently in the mother tongue. Of course, once they've served their time in Coláiste Colmchroí or Lorcain, or wherever, they'll be stuck straight into the hallowed halls of fortune that Mum or Dad attended to claim their rightful place at Ireland's top table. A primary education *as Gaeilge* no longer marks you as a nationalist or an idealist, but as one of the chosen ones, assigned to guide a new breed of Gaels through the twenty-first century, a century these children will shape here and abroad, all the time sure of their Celtic lore and willing to give motivational speeches in their native language should the need arise.

If you haven't the foresight to sign up for a place in one of these establishments while still in the delivery ward, or the political presence or cashflow to ensure acceptance, you can always opt for the Educate Together. They may not have the lingo but they have the right attitude and are far fresher than those smelly regular schools.

There's no such thing as 'Mr Murphy' or 'Miss O'Reilly' in the ETs, it's all: 'Hi Frank, I did my Basque Social History assignment early, do you think you could mark it today and give me extra credit?' 'No problem Fabio, just leave it on my desk made from stressed oak recovered from the forest during that storm last year, and you get back to chasing signatures for your Amnesty petition. Oh, and by the way, any hints on what you'd like for your birthday? You're only six once, y'know.' 'Hey, don't worry about it Frank, your presence will be enough for a kid like me, but maybe you could throw in a goat for a hungry family in Africa.' 'Sure thing dude. High five.'

But you have to be quick to get into an ET because their portacabins and prefabs fill up fast. They may be hothousing the liberals of tomorrow but they're not getting much cash from government. If you miss the ET window of opportunity it'll be down to the national with you to sign up with Sr Mary Joseph and start saving for that communion party. God bless.

MEETING THE PRINCIPAL AFTER THIRTY YEARS

You're a grown man, consummate professional, you deal with other professionals every day, you make deals and you break hearts, you've been through good times and bad and you have the scars to prove it. Not much phases you. You like to think of yourself as charming and fair, politically and environmentally aware, astute in business and engaging in society. You are as comfortable playing a round at a fundraiser in the K Club as you are urging on the under-nine hurlers from the sideline. In your own head, men admire you and women desire you.

Armed with your gold exterior and polished manners you advance to the Principal's office to introduce the first product of your loins, the child that will surely put this school on the map. You knock on the door.

'Come in.'

You enter and there she is. A rather thin woman, upright and self-contained, pressed in behind a desk that's slightly too small in a room that's slightly too big. She's marking something but stands up and extends her hand.

You follow suit, march over and shake, saying, 'Hi, I'm Martin McArdle.' You give her the 100 watt beamer. Her hand is cool and dry.

'I'm Ms Doyle.' Emphasis on the 'Ms'.

Your knees buckle slightly and you're conscious of a mist on your forehead. You signal to your daughter, 'This is Jane. She's very excited about coming here in September, aren't you Jane?'

Jane stares at the Principal open-eyed, agog. This is not the impression you wanted her to give. Where is her sparkle?

'Maybe Jane would like to go play in the yard while Daddy and I speak,' suggests Ms Doyle, 'There's a brand new slide out there and a climbing frame.' Jane turns and immediately leaves the room. No questions asked, order received and followed. For the first time ever.

You realise the power of the physical entity you are sharing oxygen with. She turns her gaze on you. 'Sit, Martin, sit,' she says.

For the next fifteen minutes she informs you of the school's policy, its ethos, its attitude to bullying and racism, its sporting, musical and dramatic traditions, its ICT infrastructure, its involvement in exchange programmes, its place in the community. Then she takes you on a whirlwind tour. Finally, 'Any questions, Martin?'

You rack your brains for something smart to say, 'No, Ms Doyle, that all seems perfectly, ahm, good.'

'Very well then. School starts on September 1st and finishes early for Junior Infants that day. Ensure she has her book list money and a snack. Until then, good day, and enjoy your summer.'

And you find yourself outside, sucking down gulps of air, relieved, as if you've gotten away with something. You spy Jane hanging from a bar and call over, 'C'mon honey, let's go home.'

'No, Daddy, I want to stay.'

A cool voice emanates from the window behind you, 'Jane, Daddy said it's time to go.'

Jane drops and runs over. You both head for the gate. Once into the car you turn to her and ask, 'So, what do you think of your new school, honey?'

'It's okay I suppose. The yard is cool.'

'Did you like Ms Doyle?'

'She's okay I suppose. Did you like her, Daddy? She was talking to you for a while.'

'Oh yes, she seemed like a very nice lady. And she loves the school and she wants all the kids to do really well. She'll take such good care of you and she told me your teacher's name is Miss Elliot. All the kids love her.'

'Okay, Daddy.'

You drive home and she forgets about school for that last summer before she belongs to it.

You can be a head of state, an open-heart surgeon, an Olympic gold medal winner, but when you cross that threshold again you're nine years old and you've been caught enjoying your first ciggie behind the bike sheds. Nothing shrivels your mickey like the dry tones and assured presence of a primary school principal. Back in the day she was a 'headmistress' but I can only presume that label was ditched in favour of the other title as it is applicable to either gender. Maybe 'Mistress' conjured up images of Elvira and domination among pre-teen boys and causing consternation and confused urges. Either way, the Principal is most assuredly still the Headmistress.

And you are still a little boy.

SUDDENLY THEY'RE NICE AGAIN AND YOU DON'T WANT THEM TO GO

A letter arrives through the door containing a circular with details of holiday dates for the forthcoming school year, a book list and uniform requirements. There are fleeting memories of your mother dragging you into Arnotts to have you suited and booted but aside from that this is the first time you've been involved in the administration of education. You look at your child who may be hanging upside down from a swing-set in the back garden or chewing the head off an action man and realise you're kitting them out for war.

School, eh? It comes flooding back, the itchy pants, the classroom, the kid beside you who hasn't yet learned to wipe his nose, roaming through the yard in packs, ruled copybooks with never-ending pages of pencilled lower case letters, learning your place in the jungle. The first place you let go of the exact whereabouts of your parents. Your first place.

Shit, she's gone. The child in the back garden hunting for snails, the one who has been glued to your leg for four years, who you gave up any thought of independent living for, is off to see the world. Part of you reaches for the Bollinger and the other half collapses in a demoralised, remorseful mess. You know you have to pull yourself together but every sentimental movie you've sat through suddenly pales into insignificance as you're hit with a dose of Class A schmaltz and you yearn for your kiddie back. As reality re-grips, you know that this will pass, you know that spending time with them will soon have you begging for space and once again looking forward to emptying them out into someone else's care.

Wrong. They know, somehow, that you've gone soft and instead of heading straight for the jugular, as they usually would, they decide to comfort and console you by becoming the most charming, entertaining and loving child a father could hope for. Rather than scream around the house with a bucket of gloss paint to adorn your new carpets and fresh walls, they will settle at the kitchen table with their crafts set and carefully construct delicate artefacts to present to you. And as they do so, they'll tell you how much they love you.

They can push every button.

You're thinking about the extra cash you'll have in your pocket when you don't have to worry about childcare costs. You're thinking about the new friends they'll make who will invite them to spend long afternoons wrecking their houses. Those same friends will never, of course, cross your threshold. You're thinking about school trips and sports and drama and all the things that'll occupy them and tire them out and have them so exhausted that when they come home all they'll want to do is hug you and climb into bed. You're thinking about time, that most valuable of commodities that was snatched from your grasping fingers the moment you witnessed that head crown between their mother's thighs. It's all there for you, languid hours studying the form, taking in international events and preparing to become a bar-room economics bore. And you don't want it back because the beast that snatched it away in the first place has suddenly become a human being, with thoughts not just for its own well-being, but also those around it.

During this summer before school you can take them places, the cinema, the circus, the swimming pool, and their number one priority will not be to escape your clutches and throw themselves kamikaze style down the nearest escalator or into the jaws of a waiting lion. No, they'll hold your hand and take in what's going on and afterwards they'll want to talk to you about what they saw. They'll be enthusiastic and excited and thank you for the effort you put in to ensuring they had a good time. They'll be grateful and harmonious and endearing, and parents all around you will acknowledge what a perfect child you have and nod with an implicit understanding that you are the fully-realised parent. They want your kids and they want to be you. For a brief period in time you are Brad Pitt and Angelina Jolie.

Married to that is their growing concern at going to school. They begin to become anxious, not at the thought of what awaits them beyond those gates, but at leaving you. Even their anxiety becomes poignant as opposed to irritating as they continue to tell you that all they want is to hang with you because you are the best dad in the world to hang with. Just before they go to school, you attain the perfect parent-child relationship. Because the world is a cruel place and thrives on making jokes of our lives. For the previous four years you either harked back to your newly-glamorised single life or looked forward to a time of peace when you could pack them out the door. With nature's cruel twist, that is taken from you and you become the tear-soaked loser at the gates on the first day of school.

REGAINING YOUR SENSES AND YOUR FREEDOM

Get a grip of yourself, man, you can always breed more if it all becomes too much. It would make better financial sense to realise that school really doesn't free up much spare time, in fact it places extra demands on your time, and the momentary glimpse you had of the angel child is blown away as they embrace playground culture. So, as Mike Skinner says, 'Dry your eyes, mate,' and get on with raising the funds to keep them up with the classroom Joneses.

While you watch the crocodile line snake into the classroom on the first morning, cast an eye over the other parents witnessing their offspring trail off on their maiden voyage, for this is your crew for the next eight years. Take note of the similarly wet first-timers and the hardened bruisers who have been through this before. Make eye contact and smile because the playground extends to you too. You can be sure every little detail is being taken in, how you're dressed, what car you drive, how you sneak in a quick smoke once you're out the gates. The child is gone, into a new world, and seemingly unnoticed you have entered one too.

Chapter 15

Getting Your Game Back

SKIN, HAIR, CLOTHES—REMEMBER THEM?

As you turn away from the school gates that first morning a number of thoughts will run through your head, the usual suspects, like wondering if she'll survive and stuff and hoping that you won't bleat until you're out of sight of everyone else. You might catch sight of yourself in a shop window as you retreat and it could be worth your while taking note of what you see.

If the descriptive words that spring to mind include shrunken, sunken, receding, shoddy, grey or bent, then it could be worth considering an extreme father makeover. EFM's don't compare to the shows on telly where fat women averse to the gym, with a penchant for lard and severe emotional problems, get to spend six months undergoing plastic surgery only to emerge at the end and marvel at the shape they've been chiselled into. No, your basic EFM involves scraping the vomit from your lapel and learning to stand up straight again, but it is amazing what a difference this can make.

From the birth we spend most of our time bent over, either lifting a child up or placing it back down. We raise to appease or clean or feed, and we replace to sleep or when we can do nothing else and need to walk away. As the child grows, our load grows because we continue to lift long after they need us to. When we're not lifting we're leaning into washing machines or dryers or dishwashers, or we're peering into a bottom shelf in a supermarket because you're sure that hidden there is the one jar of food that the child will design to eat. We begin to move into the garden and bend to examine the lumpen lawnmower and pull up weeds. We have no interest in growing anything, we simply want to appear busy somewhere by ourselves. We have read our parenting bibles and know that to discipline a child one should always go to their height so as not to tower over them intimidatingly, and so we bend. We bend, bend, bend. We bend over and take it.

Think back to the other first-morning parents. What a stooped and crippled bunch, all bent double to kiss and hug their respective sprogs goodbye. Why can't *they* jump up, or buy stilts? Shortarses.

In just four or five years you have developed a hunch and you're possibly wearing clothing you bought before the birth. If there's any hair left on your crown it has thinned or greyed, and your pot belly is mirrored by the roll on your back as well as a swollen chin. Your face is grey, a riot of broken veins, disturbed by the etched lines which you're pretty sure have only recently sunken their imprints.

Everyone ages, there's no secret there. But we shouldn't age twenty years in five. Most of us would have fancied ourselves a bit at some point, some more than others and most undeservedly so, but now we look in the mirror and see some decrepit old wino peer back. It doesn't have to be this way, nor does it have to stay this way forever. Address the problem. Focus on the yummiest mummy in the yard, the one who reputedly worked at Stringfellows. She got knocked up at seventeen, making her twenty-two now. She's obviously not going to give your tubby arse a second glance, but make it your mission to catch her noticing you at least once in the coming academic year. It will make the drop-off or pick-up every day that small bit more agreeable.

For a start, buy some decent clobber. You're not going to get all street massive and start rolling with the homies but there's no excuse for maintaining the corduroy and tweed grandad look. Every father suffers the fall into sartorial despair when each designer shirt has been soiled by bodily fluid, but those projectile days should be past now. It's time to start looking good. Take the saved former childcare money and invest in a casual suit and some

Italian shoes, think Strellson and Dior. But before you get clothed, something will have to be done about that washed-out, haunted face.

Either buy some moisturiser, any old Boots crap will make a dent, or if you really want to treat up book yourself an appointment for a facial and throw in a full body massage while you're at it. If anyone asks, insist the appointment was a present ... from the missus for last Christmas, and you stuck the voucher in a drawer and forgot all about it. Only when you're smooth and oiled and stinking of witch-hazel will the clothes maketh the man. To mark the rite of passage have somebody shave you and adjust, minimally, your ten-year-old hairstyle, such as it is. Take your first manicure, or at the very least clip the hangnails and give yourself a scrub. Fresh face, fresh hair, suited and booted—your hunch will miraculously disappear and you may rediscover a little swagger in that strut.

Of course, all this will count for little if you have a Body Mass Index of 35 and the muscle tone of Christopher Biggins. It's time to start giving serious thought to exercise again. Don't kid yourself that you were ever any good at football, it's every mid-thirties geezer's bullshit nostalgia. You were crap back in the day and you'd be worse now should you be stupid enough to attempt to pull the boots on again after a decade gathering dust. You're fat and you're unfit. Start easy, walk a few miles, build it up into a jog four times a week, get in the pool or on a bike. Play some tag rugby with a bunch of other talentless ex-pretend jocks in a public park as long as girls are involved too. They'll remind you not to over-exert. But most of all, work up a sweat and remind yourself that you weren't born to be the pig you've turned into.

MAKING LIKE A PLAYER—WHERE'S YOUR ATTITUDE?
The thing about kids is they pressure you into being nice. Nice is important with kids, you can't expect to develop a meaningful relationship with them if you arrive at the breakfast table with: 'Yo, homies, wassup bitches? You betta be makin them Cheerios disappear or there's gonna be some whupass administered in this

here kitchen. What's a man gotta do to get some pancakes in this house? Come on bitch, this ain't no theme park. Serve yo man.' No, the south-central LA, straight outta Compton school of parenting and husbandry never took off in respectable suburbs.

Instead we learn to serve. When you're feeding, dressing and cleaning another human being constantly over a period of time your altruistic streak needs to strengthen for the family unit to survive. Also, there seems to be a proportionate decline in our own self-care as we look after the needs of others. If you're going to start looking good you might as well introduce a little attitude. There's no need to mail order a bunch of gold chains and get your local barber to insert corn rows, but there's no harm in toughing up a little. Everybody likes a nice guy, you remember the one back in school, all the girls used to talk about him, 'Ah, Ken's so nice, he's lovely.' But none of them shagged him. You don't want to be that guy.

Okay, being straight with the kids is a prerequisite, you like them after all. They expect a high level of care and you provide their role model. It's when 'niceness' starts seeping into your work and your social life that things begin to get confused. Your friends got to know you, and possibly like you, when you behaved like a hooligan. They get confused when suddenly you start to display concern at their problems. When they admit difficulties with their girlfriends and, instead of pouncing on them and referring to their obvious inadequacies in the sack, you start to quiz them about their feelings and the levels of communication in their relationship, they don't know how to respond. They'll never come to you with problems again if you offer advice: they get that from girls. They expect you to rip the piss and lighten the mood. It's no wonder nobody's been calling you recently.

As for the office, ever wondered why you've been passed over for that promotion both times one has come up in the last two years? You're strolling up and down corridors offering people coffee and remembering to bring in cards on birthdays. Nobody knows where they stand with all this sincerity floating around. The fact that you've streamlined administration procedures and implemented a new marketing policy doesn't spark admiration in your colleagues, it makes them fearful, as if they might be expected to follow suit. For years you refused to raise a finger beyond the exact terms of your job description and you did fine because everyone knew what was going on in your head. Now you're rocking the boat with all this proactive nonsense. Maybe it's time to kick back at your desk and get a bit jobsworthy, to use the best facilities management speak—concentrate on your 'core process'. It will relieve the pressure on those around you, free up some time to do some decent bitching about colleagues and the boss, and probably result in a promotion.

IT'S ONLY BEEN FIVE YEARS BUT YOU'VE WOKEN UP A GENERATION LATER

The night before you headed for the delivery ward you were still the last of your line. In your family, you were the kid, exuberant with youthful charm, wild and wonderful, daring and dangerous. Because you were the kid, you still had potential, but potential can be a terrible thing.

Applying for a job in your twenties is very different to applying for one in your thirties. At twenty-five you have to convince a prospective employer that you could be great. You will be bought on the basis of your enthusiasm, hunger and drive. Potential. At thirty-five you have to convince a prospective employer that you're not shit. You dress up the previous ten years' work to appear like you cut a swathe through junior and middle management but the fact is you are in a mid-level role, applying for a bit of a jump that might allow you to buy a house with another bedroom and a larger garden. Potential is gone, replaced by average. Dreams of world domination and private jets fade as the reality of car loans and the possibility of leather in your next mid-range Jap sedan take hold. You work. You pay the man.

On the night before the birth, you were the kid. A day later you were the dad. It happened that fast—all the potential transferred from you to the child, and your job became the funding and management of that potential. You didn't realise it at the time, but

after a while you look up and twig that you are no longer the star
of the family, you are the star's facilitator. You are the middle
generation, in familial terms, middle management. You bear the
stress and deal with administration while the generations on either
side of you get to kick back and soak up the good times.

You can go to the gym, run a few marathons, buy some clobber,
throw your weight around in the office, get your groove back, but
you're never going to pilot your own space shuttle to the moon. Or
as Marianne Faithfull sang:

> 'At the age of thirty-seven she realised she'd never
> Ride through Paris in a sports car with the warm wind in
> her hair.'[11]

Poor old Lucy Jordan. But the rest of us muddle on and it's not so
much the realisation that we are now mid-generation and so a step
ahead of kids that is shocking, more that in the adult world we
have moved into the realm of mid-generation and so are distinct
from young adults. Those who can still afford to spend the
majority of their income on lager and Ibiza.

Before the birth there was no real distinction between you and
anyone else. Now you find yourself having been shifted in the work
canteen from the singles' table to the parents' table. You don't
know when this happened but it dawns on you that you've been
sitting there a while. Over lunch, talk focuses on credit problems,
house prices and school nativity plays. You look longingly over at
the other table where the buxom new receptionist is howling about
how she broke one of her heels on the steps down to a basement
nightclub on Leeson Street last Friday night. You make to get up
and join them but realise you can't, you are welded to where you
are as surely as if you had shackles round your ankles. Buxom
receptionist is only ten feet away but you will never sit beside her.
Shut up and eat your ham roll.

ACCEPTING THE CHANGE AND EMBRACING YOUR INNER AULD FELLA!

It's all a bit of a relief really, letting your younger self go. It's the mental equivalent of accepting the woollen cardigan as a Christmas present and being surprised to find it really is comfortable. And warm. And hang it all, if people want to start calling you Daniel O'Donnell—this is a fine cardie.

Being the kid is tough going. You have the burden of all that potential, all those expectations that you're the one, the Highlander. You have to be charming and witty, you have to excel at work and on the sportsfield, you have to be out and about all the time working hard so everybody knows you're a contender. Jaysus, with all that pressure, having the baby comes as a relief. You can hide out indoors for months, years even, and when you emerge nobody expects a whole lot any more. Hi, I'm Joe Average, mind if I kick back here?

So, say you've pulled yourself together and are once again walking upright in reasonable togs without your knuckles dragging along the ground, there are any number of pluses to your predicament making it more attractive than your old, single, playboy days.

1. Slippers. Like the cardigan, slippers are a luxury you cannot afford as a single man. Score on a Saturday night? Just about to close the deal with some choice moves back at your place? She spots your brown check pair with fleece innards poking out from under the bed and suddenly realises she's left the oven on at home. Once you have kids, slippers are obligatory. Bliss.

2. Parking. Stick a baby chair in the back seat and you get privileges in all supermarkets and multi-storeys.

3. Your waistline. Oh man, ease it out. Pop the top button on your Levi's after those bhajis, samosas, vindaloos, pizzas, quarter pounders, batter burgers, spring rolls, three-in-one boxes, chicken wings, Ben & Jerry's, tubes of Pringles, chocolate éclairs, wontons, barbequed ribs, and turkey and cranberry sauce sandwiches. Let your belly rumble in comfort. Slap it and watch the waves roll in.

4. Admitting you don't give a toss about wine—you drink it if you want to get shitfaced in a hurry. In the beginning, when impressing people was a concern, you had to make noises about bouquet and body. Now you're free to drain a bottle and crash it over a wine bore's head.

5. Friday night TV. You can watch *The Late Late Show* without being ironic, although you might want to keep it to yourself. You also have Jonathan Ross to entertain you and whatever Channel 4 is selling. No longer is it obligatory to spend weekend nights in overcrowded, overpriced boozers. You can pick and choose where and when you want to piss away your cash.

6. SUVs. Yeah, come on feel my power! Carbon footprint, what carbon footprint? Kids come along and provide the perfect excuse for purchasing a 6-litre, v8 behemoth that defies the Kyoto Agreement on its own. If there's any risk someone else's motor might crush yours then it's only right that you should have the biggest beast in town. It's for the kiddies, not to feed your monster truck fetish. Oh yeah.

7. Golf. You don't have to play any more. You have an in-built excuse not to stride around elitist, manicured, misogynist clubs with a bunch of colour-blind, sartorially challenged, chinless gimps in the name of networking. Watch cartoons with your three-year-old instead.

8. Animated films. Admit it, you wanted to see *Toy Story* in the cinema and the *Shrek* series is the twenty-first century's answer to *The Godfather* trilogy. Load up on popcorn and corn chips and get down with Disney and Pixar. No more pretending you care about German Arthouse.

9. Education. Soak up the admiration as the kids marvel at your ability to add double digit numbers. Who cares if you don't know your Camille Paglia from your Virginia Wolfe? All you need is, 'Who's afraid of the big, bad wolf?'

10. The brats themselves. The fruit of your loins. The summation of your seed. The culmination of your copulation. They're quite nice, we like having them around.

The first time I heard the phrase 'The Daddy' I was watching Ray Winstone in Alan Clarke's *Scum*. Winstone asserted his authority in a violent borstal by battering senseless the boy who had previously run the show. As he stood over his adversary's prostrate form and delivered kick after kick, the young Winstone repeatedly asked him, 'Who's the Daddy now then, eh?'

None of us is living the savage life of thuggery the kids in that film endured, but the phrase they adopted for the top boy was 'The Daddy'. That says something. I am the Daddy, you are the Daddy. We may be reasonably rotund, a bit bet down, we may never light up the sky and have a punk soundtrack written for the movie to our lives, we may prefer reading C.S. Lewis to a captive audience of an evening rather than schmoozing in the latest celebrity nightclub, but you better tread carefully because there's a bit of 'The Daddy' in all of us. If something or someone threatens those close to us they'll soon find out we can still throw a few slaps.

Because the kids mean everything. They define us in a way that nothing else does, not our jobs, our social lives or our friends. They remind us how close we are to the earth we live on, because we've been there from their bloody entrance and stood beside them ever since. Mortgages, careers, romances, addictions, they may all have clouded the fact that we're scrubbing around down here in the muck, but the kids remind us of how thin the veil between us and the wild is.

They remind us that we are somebody, and like 'The Daddy' we have to stand up. They give us that present every day.

Notes

1. Breastfeedingfacts.com

2. serf. (n.d.). *The American Heritage® Dictionary of the English Language, Fourth Edition.* Retrieved 10 April 2008, from Dictionary.com website: *http://dictionary.reference.com/browse/serf*

3. www.sleep-deprivation.com

4. 'This Be The Verse' from *High Windows* by Philip Larkin, reproduced by permission of Faber and Faber Ltd.

5. http://www.ivillage.co.uk/parenting/occasions/birthdays/articles/0,,637040
   _639173,00.html

6. http://marriage.about.com/od/sex/i/fantasies_2.htm

7. http://www.babycentre.co.uk/toddler/pottytraining/whenchildready/

8. Nassim Nicholas Taleb, *The Black Swan, The Impact of the Highly Improbable,* (Penguin 2007), p. 27.

9. http://kidshealth.org/parent/emotions/feelings/sibling_rivalry.html

10. Thanks to Chapter One and Restaurant Patrick Guilbaud, both of Dublin, for their menu listings.

11. 'The Ballad of Lucy Jordan', Marianne Faithfull, page 208.